A STYLE AND ITS ORIGINS

HOWARD BARKER/EDUARDO HOUTH

A STYLE AND ITS ORIGINS

OBERON BOOKS
LONDON

First published in 2007 by Oberon Books Ltd.

521 Caledonian Road, London N7 9RH

Tel: 020 7607 3637 / Fax: 020 7607 3629

info@oberonbooks.com / www.oberonbooks.com

A Style and its Origins © copyright Howard Barker 2006, 2007

Reprinted in 2012

Howard Barker is hereby identified as author of this work in accordance with section 77 of the Copyright, Designs and Patents Act 1988. The author has asserted his moral rights.

A catalogue record for this book is available from the British Library.

ISBN: 1 84002 718 5 / 978-1-84002-718-1

Cover photograph by Eduardo Houth

Printed in Great Britain by Antony Rowe Ltd., Chippenham

I do these things
Oh how I persist I am at least persistent

And I ask
Does anybody want them?

The answer comes back
Nobody at all

So I go on

Howard Barker, *The Forty*

'*Art is a form of knowledge: it expresses through its autonomy what is concealed by the empirical form of reality…*'

'*Only those thoughts are true which fail to understand themselves*'

Theodor Adorno, *Notes On Literature*

Preface

FOR TWENTY YEARS I KEPT NOTES. I thrust the notes into a box. I wanted to write about Barker but when I came to the box the chaos inside it dismayed me. I could not organise the parts coherently or smooth the contradictions. This angered me until I understood that the disorder of the box was precisely how I had experienced the work of Barker and the poet himself, that it was the essence of him and that to place order on it would be to do violence to it and in effect, distort the character of this complex artist and his creations. For all his adult life Barker kept a detailed and intimate journal. For those who would know him, they might look there. Here I give what are my impressions of a man whose passions and attitudes I became familiar with, admired and came to understand.

For all that he struggled to impose order on his life Barker's mind was unruly, swimming in currents of passion, prejudice, history and love. He thought his time sordid and suffered an emotional and physical distaste for it, preserving his ecstasies for the spiritual and sexual life he created for himself. He craved solitude. He was thin-skinned. Neither quality befits a man of the theatre, where bruising is routine. So he invented a method, as an alternative to flight or suicide. This book might show how that method came to be.

Barker's intense dissatisfaction with what theatre had achieved extended to himself. He thought theatre did not go far enough, and he thought the same of himself. But further where? Just as when a child he destroyed so much that he was simultaneously proud of so as a mature artist he found even in his finest work failure and imperfection, whilst painfully aware that imperfection was entirely characteristic of achievement itself. His imagination expressed itself in many and contradictory forms: in his painting, in his set and costume designs, a severe, monochromatic discipline imposed itself. The sets of Tomas Leipzig for the Wrestling School are distinguished by their economy and beauty, Billy Kaiser's costumes by their stylish regime of *haute couture*. To those who saw *Und*, few can forget the disturbing spectacle of the unoccupied set, the steel tray flying on long rods of steel with the rhythm of an industrial machine, its tea service awesomely still while a trickle of sand, wavering, dropped from on high to create a mound on the pierced floor, uncanny signs of absences... If this was him in his refined austerity, his plays overflowed with a deliberate excess, even in their various forms, from the great extent of *The Ecstatic Bible* with its hundred-charactered cast and cascade of settings, to the cruel and oppressive interiors of *Isonzo* or *A House Of Correction*, from half-histories like *Victory* to the painful bettering of Shakespeare's sexualities in *Gertrude – The Cry*.

Sometimes we read our poems in little rooms to audiences of young actors who revered him and begged him to explain what they found revelatory but simultaneously infuriatingly obscure in his work, puzzled by the contradiction that was the essence of him. He answered with a further contradiction, not out of mischief, but because his whole sense of life – which was redeemed by passion rather than love – repudiated the reduction to single meanings that culture demands as due payment for its tolerance... in this he demanded they ask more of life than they either expected or had been taught.

E H

Madrid, 2005

I

The women of his family had been laundresses and his mother wanted to wash...

She pegged great sheets on lines and the sheets cracked in the breeze...

She sang songs from the war as she carried the basket on her hip her labour was pleasure she laughed at the wind and showed her teeth...

Barker wanted to film the simple scene as every artist in his maturity discovers this need to know what made him, the long-awaited moment when memory and the possibility of art at last collide, a perfection but a brevity before nostalgia sets in and rots integrity...

In his play *He Stumbled* Barker directed the actors in a scene with a washing-line and a laundry basket... he wanted the action of pegging out washing to be continuous, an element of the seduction that followed from the intimacy of this domestic activity. He wanted it to begin with the sheet, wet and heavy from the wash. He asked the actors to find the ends and to pull the sheet between them with short, co-ordinated movements to cause the creases to fall out before it could be suspended from the line. Neither actor recognised or understood this routine, known and natural to Barker from his infancy, and when they learned it mechanically it did not satisfy him. He insisted on the rhythm that came from familiarity. When they had achieved this, and only then, the actors began to laugh foolishly and frequently dropped the sheet or pulled it from one another's hands. Barker knew they had fulfilled the obligation of the moment, for whilst he insisted they should not drop the sheet, he knew from his childhood that both he and his mother giggled helplessly on nearly every occasion they carried out this operation, it was intrinsic to it and a crucial element of the seduction...

In *The Castle* Stucley finds sinister presentiments of approaching disaster in the state of his linen

I sleep alone in sheets grey with tossing, I cannot keep
a white sheet white, do you find this? Grey by the
morning. The launderers are frantic.

The rectangle of pristine white, the bedsheet or the starched tablecloth, features routinely in his painting and in his plays... Tenna scattering the knives and forks so meticulously polished by the palace servant in *Animals In Paradise* and replacing the cutlery with her own body... the dazzling shroud of *Dead Hands*, a literal whitening of a dark secret... the tablecloth laid with infinite care by Photo, the blind protagonist of *The Fence In Its Thousandth Year*, as he picnics beside barbed wire, innocence neighbouring cruelty...

Barker talked of '*the shock of cleanliness*' on the stage... the white sheet has for him a perverse value, like the white bridal costume which demands to be desecrated in his rewritten *Women Beware Women*, or the dazzling white gown which is fouled in *Und*... in his painting the white forms of suspended or draped sheets act as an immaculate commentary on the sordid facts of the social world... the naked patronne relaxes in her empty café among a maze of tablecloths in *La Patronne At 1 a.m.*... like tents white shapes surround the *Dead Russian Soldier By The Yalu River* or hang from lines in rows in *The Threadbare Flags Of Surrender*, and in the self-portrait with Victoria Wicks *We Fail To Sell Ourselves Even* the figures pose before white canvasses slung from a shop front...

Barker wrote on paper, never on the electronic screen, and affirmed his love of the paper sheet by only ever using the larger obsolescent kind known as foolscap, long abolished by the manufacturers... they searched for this paper... a unique supply was discovered in a rural place...

And on this sheet of white, the ordering of the speeches so peculiar to Barker, the lines separated according to their rhythms of

Word
Placed
Under
Word

to indicate the burden of pain with which each syllable is to be uttered, a discipline bewildering to actors until they spoke and then self-evident. In this as in so much with Barker's texts things lucid only with the act of articulation...

2

BARKER SPOKE OF HIS CHILDHOOD but mostly as sound... with the fall of darkness deep-breathing locomotives slipping on the incline from their too-heavy freights...the trucks elbowing one another as they clattered back... over it the screaming of out-late girls... under it the boy-shouts... with dawn the plaintive convent bell disputing with the factory hooters calling women workers to the assembly line... it was profoundly urban yet from his window he saw ancient trees... his family had been rehoused as a consequence of overcrowding and their asbestos prefab stood on a park... the park had been pasture in another century... where they lived in tight proximity is grass again... Barker called his poems excavations and thought of London not as wide but deep... his sense of the dispersal of all things runs through his work... accumulations both spiritual and material cannot resist decay... in an early play situated on the cemeteries of the Great War the iconoclastic Lalage says of the unborn generations

> *They will forget. They will eat sandwiches here and*
> *bring their dogs to shit*
>
> (*The Love Of A Good Man*)

And the witch Skinner envisions the casual ignorance of the future as it treads over the sacred sites of the past, the scene of her own ordeal, and the dreadful edifice which initiated it, all subject to the law of oblivion

This floor, laid over flowers we once lay on, this cruel
floor will become the site of giggling picnics, clots of
children wandering with music in their ears and not
one will think, not one, A WOMAN WRITHED HERE
ONCE.

(The Castle)

Barker's family exerted on him a simultaneous anxiety
and rage... nature was threatening, society a conspiracy
of thieves... if his mother described the first out of a
suffocating love, his father articulated the second from an
impassioned communism learned in the war and exercised
on the factory floor... neither spared him love... he called
his father a beautiful man and heard him always calling in
his sons

It was heard
And it was kind the paternal voice
Softened by the kitchen's sweltering
Boy come in:
So out of the gloved dark he walked
Humped with secrecy
His thin bones marrowed with small crime

Barker's father lived the demise of the socialist idea and it
injured him, just as his mother suffered the decay of public
loyalty to the uncomplicated patriotism that had made
soldiers and sailors of her family... their quarrels had been
the constant antiphony to Barker's infant years, a grinding
more pitiful than cruel, and he ached for them...

Now let me rest my ancestors
The light bones the hair clouds
The brittle shaft of an idea
Whose iron head fell from its
Reiterations

A dense body of his early plays describes the dying of the socialist ethic – so hard a weapon, so liable to rust – and in the end he could no longer participate in the elaboration of the progressive theory that underlay so much of the European theatre of his time – his repudiation of it was visceral, but in theatre he articulated its irrelevance, its negativity, even its morbidity in theoretical texts like *Arguments* and *Death, The One*... he called all the arts of morality timid, conformist and made from a substance he thought poisonous in both life and art – shame... much later he was able to write, from a profound despair

There is need for terrible dying and of grief
For the many dead
That the coming through might learn silence
And stare at their bread for minutes on end

Observing his timidity as a child and apprehensive for him, Barker's mother urged him to learn the arts of sociability, to become 'one of the boys'... primitively she knew the power of the male collective, but he preferred the company of women young and old... when Barker fell into the theatre – a place where the collective of the boys never ceases to wield a dominant authority – she tried to buy his first play from him to keep it from being staged...

As a child he heard her sexual cries through the cardboard wall... his bed lay against it and in the darkness he fretted that she was ill or dreaming terrible dreams... why did his father not comfort her...? Always the contradiction wounded him... later the woman's cry became for him a thing of infinite significance as it is for all men more or less... and the philosophical basis for his greatest play...

He carried his father's ashes through the streets where he had spent his life...

After the death of his mother he never visited South London again...

3

BARKER DID NOT INVENT The Wrestling School but he gave it its name... in this name lay intuitions both personal and public... for him theatre was a place of struggle and of domination, as the playground is a place of fear and noise... he knew his plays were called difficult and called them so himself, arguing that difficulty was a price to pay if not for enlightenment – which he cared nothing for – then for spiritual experience... and he knew much of this perceived difficulty arose simply because his plays did not obey the rules of the dominant aesthetic... they observed other rules... his own... the name was suggestive also of those secret societies which during the Fascist period had concealed themselves under innocuous names and Barker thought of his theatre as a secret... the more so as the age became obsessively transparent and threatened to eliminate the private sphere...

Kenny Ireland, an actor and a man of discernment who concealed his pity under a volatile foam of conviviality and violence – a character therefore profoundly sympathetic to Barker – came to Barker's home on a summer's afternoon with Hugh Fraser, another actor familiar with his work, both men discontents... They perched in Barker's small, high study and asked him for a play. Both of them had seen Barker's conversion of Middleton's Jacobean classic *Women Beware Women* and wanted a similar violation perpetrated on Chekhov... Barker felt an antipathy for Chekhov which later materialised in his *(Uncle) Vanya* but at this time he wanted only to write original plays and suggested a new work about the death of Christ. The actors trusted his instinct... the play became *The Last Supper*...

There was an infectious spirit of ambition... whilst they talked of the one play Barker already thought of it as only the first... he asked about buildings... seasons of work... prolific as he was he thought it necessary to keep up a stream of productions in order to familiarise the public with the different values they embodied... Ireland was patient, sharing his pleasure but a realist first and pragmatic... he had directed Barker's *Power Of The Dog* for the Joint Stock Theatre group, a theatre company Barker disdained, thinking its passion for relevance pitiful and vain. The same group had mounted his *Victory* after it had languished at the Royal Court, ignored. In both cases, the production of an existing text was expedient. The Joint Stock Theatre group's existence was predicated on a working method which dispensed with the writer as the imaginative source and invested instead in research and workshop. The failure of a project obliged them to reach for an existing text. Ireland had played the furious cavalier in *Victory*, Fraser the Soviet NKVD officer in *The Power Of The Dog*… furthermore, both had played Barker in their period with the RSC and both shared a perception that his plays had never yet been properly seen… that there was a *way* with them yet to be articulated… but whilst Barker spoke freely of the elitism innate in new artistic practice such as his own, Ireland saw qualities in his work of a sufficiently popular kind to generate a bigger audience. With strong direction and an ensemble spirit, Ireland was convinced he could remove the stigma of 'difficulty' from Barker. He was immediately presented with a text that put this faith to the test. *The Last Supper* remained one of Barker's favourite plays, the narrative punctuated with parables, the theme violently manipulated, and the whole prefaced by a prologue which succinctly stated Barker's contempt for a social-realist theatre. By dint of his own efforts Ireland placed this act of mutiny on the stage of the Royal Court Theatre, in effect a brilliant stroke of *lèse-majesté*. The critical and public response was indifferent. Philip Sayer, whose personification of Barker's vain and mercurial Christ – here known as Lvov, a fortuitous invocation of love and an ancient Polish city, a highly Barkerian naming – had represented a triumph and a vindication of Ireland's method, died a year later. He had invested himself in the role, an immense undertaking. Barker wrote in memory of Sayer

What we ask of the actor is a little thing
That he flings his life's conclusions in the air
And standing like a bride in the falling colours
Weeps with anticipation of inevitable silences

Barker knew the emotional stress his work induced in the best actors, and knew it was no little thing to submit to it. His whole attitude to the tragic experience implied an ordeal both for the performer and his public, and this ordeal became for Barker the spiritual condition of his *Theatre of Catastrophe*. In this he was already in contradiction not only to the prevailing culture of English theatre but to his own director…

4

IRELAND POSSESSED HUGE RESOURCES of energy, will and, when he required it, charm. He also simmered with physical menace. On one of many occasions when juvenile louts threatened the performance of *Victory* he had ambushed them in the aisle and caused them to blanch with horror. These were the conditions under which The Wrestling School played its work and Barker sensed the ambiguity implicit in his own method. On the one hand his manner as a writer was instinctively repelled by social realism, on the other, to escape from its suffocating miasma he was impelled towards a style which could only shock or bewilder a public now so conditioned by it as to be rendered incapable of registering its own servitude. Barker knew social realism was now degenerate. He knew it had long ago entered the entertainment phase that befalls all decayed forms. He was certain the public required a revolution but inside itself, it needed to vomit its own habit, but it was an addiction the theatre, for all that it purported to be radical, encouraged and indulged. At a conference held in Birmingham Barker spoke against the audience and was howled down. He had chosen to utter this anathema wearing a black suit. This wearing-of-a-suit compounded the offence...

> I talked about the sickness of the audience
> The democratic indignation!
> The froth of injured innocence!
> One even threatened suicide if theatre did not save
> The world...

Barker liked wool suits and recoiled from conferences, which appeared to replace practice, just as the cult of education in theatre substituted for the playing of plays... in his later designs for costumes Barker concentrated on suits of black or grey, put his actresses in hats and on an austerely beautiful stage created a milieu which emphasised the word and the status of the word-speaker...

5

BARKER HAD NO DESIRE to direct at this time. Watching Ireland at work, as he had watched William Gaskill, he sensed he had none of their talent for cruelty or control. Barker would never direct in a democratic mode, he neither asked advice nor consulted, but he was not manipulative and did not need to be since he had created the text and his authority as the interpreter of the work was beyond interrogation. Barker sensed directors were in fear of actors and in many instances disliked them. At the same time he recognised actors were frequently recalcitrant and reluctant to submit to direction, arguing every point. He knew if he were to direct it could only be with performers of a certain kind – it would need to be an ensemble united by faith, in him not only as writer, the ultimate repository of meaning, but as visualiser, delineating their position in the acting space, even the gesture and the body's attitude...

Barker was nearly always in rehearsal and Ireland's generous character did not baulk at this... most directors dread the authorial presence... Ireland wanted to serve the play and knew this required a considerable element of collaboration... on his side Barker was careful to limit his interventions... they cast the plays together and here too Ireland was tolerant and Barker not always discerning... their cohabitation on the rehearsal floor was an amicable one because Ireland had the self-confidence to permit Barker to contradict him before the actors but also the will to assert his own decisions... an uncommon talent... the mood of the rehearsal was generally ebullient and the day long, in contradistinction to the character of the rehearsal when Barker assumed control... then the atmosphere was quieter because Barker disliked anecdotes and banished news... people were more contemplative... a calmness prevailed, unconstrained... they worked intensively and the day was short...

6

BARKER NEEDED THE WRESTLING SCHOOL. He had failed to make friends in the theatre, and had cultivated few allies among critics, producers or directors. Theatres which had entertained him repudiated him. His changing aesthetic principles, articulated in newspaper articles or in his first theoretical work *Arguments For A Theatre*, served to deepen the political hostility that emanated from left and right, who are in any case united in their moral earnestness, a thing Barker was already identifying as the most serious obstacle to a new theatre. Barker was now creating texts that were challenges to the whole principle of enlightenment, as exemplified in *The Last Supper* and in short plays that his second actor-director ally Ian McDiarmid was presenting at the Almeida, *The Possibilities*. McDiarmid would soon become director of the Almeida and make of it a resounding popular success, but on terms which effectively concluded their alliance. Barker was the exile par excellence, driven by a passion incomprehensible to those like William Gaskill who had first encouraged him and whose moral and political crusades dominated their attitude to art. Barker thought too highly of theatre's powers to see them subordinated to a missionary zeal. He thought liberal humanism dead, an indecent corpse massaged by writers and critics so that it flapped its arms and legs in a miserable parody of authenticity. He had to seek out other places, and wrote plays for the darker corridors of radio, for marionettes, for opera... he wrote poetry, regularly and always at the end of the day... and he painted, as if he were using landscape as a stage...

7

IN THE FIRST INSTANCE The Wrestling School was created to perform a single work. For all Barker's faith in the idea of the permanent ensemble, the company was never permitted to enjoy the sense of security that comes with adequate funding, predicted and assured. Throughout its history it returned to the bureaucracy to plead its case. Barker's entire experience of the theatre was one of mendicancy, a fact which caused his spirit to writhe. It is the condition of all artists whose talent fails to make them wealthy. He had begun by sending his texts to theatres and attending on their decisions. Like all writers he had endured rejection and worse, the mundane justifications for the rejections, he had seen his greatest plays lie for years in the offices of theatres and nearly always it had been accident that brought them to performance. Now that a form existed under which his work might be seen outside what he was to disparage as *the theatre*, the condition of mendicancy shifted to the door of the bureaucracy. He had been delivered from the dramaturgs to the accountants...

Ireland ran The Wrestling School from his home in Fulham. He recruited a self-effacing but stubborn company manager who became expert in the arcane practices of financial procurement, Christopher Corner. Corner possessed the reservoirs of patience necessary to deal with an increasingly politicised Arts Council, thereby sustaining the work of a writer and a company whose character satisfied few if any of the ever-more rigid sociological criteria that came to be applied. After Ireland's departure Barker and Corner alone managed the company, Barker proposing the play, Corner appealing for the wherewithal. Corner was permanently discreet but frequently dismayed. He found himself making apologies for the company's style, finding it impossible to applaud those gestures that Barker increasingly employed to define and defend his aesthetic. It was a strange and unlikely relationship. Corner was obliged to satisfy the criteria imposed by his patrons, and these criteria Barker despised. Corner fretted that the audience was shrinking. Barker cared little if the public stayed away. In his heart he had a dread of their judgement. Corner implored Barker to communicate with the audience in the officially sponsored encounters between actors and public that followed performance. Barker recoiled from the proposition that such encounters should take place at all, instructing his actors to be severe in their demeanour and to avoid at all costs the anecdotal, when the anecdotal was what the public craved to hear… for Barker the experience of the performance could only be diminished by attempts at elucidation. He had nothing to teach; on the contrary his art was the antithesis of teaching. If it revealed, it was not a *show*. How could he explain what, by its essence and design, refused explanation? He submitted but looked darkly at his interrogators, some of whom in turn understood his darkness...

8

DID BARKER LIKE ACTORS? They were his only allies in theatre. The directors most associated with his work were themselves actors. His lifelong academic friend and exponent David Ian Rabey was an accomplished amateur actor, and Barker directed him in the first *Isonzo*. They responded to his text because they needed to speak, and to speak to the speech's limits. Because of this profound need in the soul of the actor, Barker loved them, but those he loved best never permitted this pure instinct to become contaminated either by vanity or the corrosive effects of the cult of entertainment. He had a vision of acting as a form of religious practice, which in its most spiritual manifestation became an ecstasy, an ecstasy in which the actor would not know himself. In this condition of ecstasy the audience would be delivered from the requirement to criticise, it would in effect be seduced into a condition of receptivity which abolished values, politics, morality from the stage and enabled it to enter the realm of authentic tragedy. Speech would not be rendered in the terms of conventional realism. Its metaphorical and rhythmic character effectively eliminated any of the associative qualities so esteemed in naturalistic theatre.

Barker did not want his audience to identify with the stage character, he required them to be overtaken by surprise and to admit surprise. His world was not the world as the realists struggled to understand it. Yet by its profound and desperate searching it surpassed the realists by its realism... not all actors possessed the capacity or the will for this practice, for its disciplines were severe and the public rewards – given the status of Barker's theatre – limited...

Barker loved two actresses and they influenced his creative life... he wrote the monologue *Und* for Melanie Jessop, and his revision of Lessing's *Minna Von Barnhelm* was made for her. Her lucent intelligence made her the perfect player for such densely-argued and combative roles. In *Ten Dilemmas* he described their mutual pain in the erotic collision of the outcasts Becker and Draper. In these and in all his later work, Barker dispensed with sympathy as a principle of his artistic practice and replaced it by a fascination with the extremes of behaviour licensed by desire or social collapse. Here were the beginnings of his *Theatre of Catastrophe*...

Later, Barker encountered Victoria Wicks...

9

HUGH FRASER PERFORMED ONLY ONCE for the company he had helped to create. His nerves had failed him for the stage, though he maintained a distinguished career elsewhere. The collapse of a member of *The Last Supper* company forced him to assume the role at desperately short notice, conspicuous in a pink suit and shuddering from terror. Barker said Fraser was transcendent, demonic, mesmerising in the role of Arnold, the disciple-cum-killer of the prophet Lvov. He had seen in Fraser's ordeal something he required of the experience of theatre – an anxiety that could be communicated, an anxiety of such intensity that it was shared by both performer and audience and which eliminated the superficial relations which characterise entertainment on the one hand and enlightenment on the other. He at once conceived for him his dissection and reanimation of Chekhov's *Uncle Vanya*, knowing the role would demand of the actor precisely his plunging horror, his nervous ambition... Fraser joined the company but quit after a week, a decision Barker deplored but could not resent...

Fraser's terror, whilst it advertised a certain form of self-consciousness, simultaneously eradicated another, that element of personal identity common to all performers but loud in the star, the 'name-actor', a thing Barker thought intruded between the character and the public's involvement with the character. He came to dislike actors – however skilled – who brought their reputations to the stage, above all those who made public their morality, who demonstrated their humanity or their charm. He found this incompatible with the playing of tragedy which he insisted demands the actor dispense with the desire to be loved and substitute instead the power of attraction, which draws on other sources. He thought few could manage this...

10

IRELAND DIRECTED *SEVEN LEARS* with many of the actors who had played *The Last Supper*, including Jane Bertish, who along with Jessop, was the only actress who worked with Ireland and, after his departure, with Barker, on a regular basis. The company came near to being a casual ensemble, but Ireland, who was more ambitious for Barker than he was for himself, and a pragmatist, wanted a substantial name for his revival of *Victory*. Barker dissented from this, believing now, as ever, that the name-actor diluted the character of the ensemble, disunited it and attracted a public for the wrong reasons. By contrast, the relative obscurity of the acting company forced attention onto the performance alone, and distinguished the audience from that which came in search of reputations. Barker had found the public for McDiarmid's *Scenes From An Execution* unsympathetic. By casting Glenda Jackson McDiarmid guaranteed full houses, but Barker queried the reasons for their attendance. For all his ostensible disregard for the audience, Barker cherished some undefined ideal of his public, one which the theatre had long ceased to address... Ireland sensed Barker needed all the help he could get but he deferred to Barker's preference for Tricia Kelly and the ensemble remained. Kelly gave a memorable performance as the wandering widow Bradshaw, stripping herself of her moral character and, in an apotheosis of transgression, sleeping with her persecutors. Ireland's production was his finest for The Wrestling School, and showed all his strengths. A lavish set by Johann Engels and music by Matthew Scott combined with Ireland's innate showmanship to produce a fluent, glamorous stage epic that almost overwhelmed the audience's moral reluctance. Ireland solved problems thrown up by the text with consummate skill – and Barker as a writer never declined to write scenes on the grounds of their staging difficulties; he assumed the director's ability to invent, substitute, compensate, as necessary, and later revealed this talent in himself. *Victory* showed the power of a dedicated company to open an apparently difficult text to a wider public and thereby fulfilled Ireland's cherished objectives. Barker and Ireland had not hesitated to talk of 'beauty' in the staging of plays, but Barker's own standards of beauty had altered. He disliked the creation of atmosphere by music, whilst embracing the idea of sound, which he used extensively in his own productions. He wanted light to sharpen the distress of scenes, by chiaroscuro effects, and he wanted costume to break the rules of authenticity, consigning colour to the edges of the palette. All that Ireland had marshalled to break through the resistance of the audience Barker sensed was inimical to the concept of theatre that was developing in him... little of this was fully apparent at the time, and Barker invited Engels and Scott to work with him in a similar way with his first production, *Hated Nightfall*. Style, Barker said, was never the superficial indulgence of taste or sensation it is frequently considered to be, but something arrived at by painful study, a distillation of thought and practice, and essentially a moral decision. In a perverse way, Barker's staging became the moral element in an imaginative world that stressed its own immorality...

11

IRELAND DID NOT FIND THE SAME FACILITY with *The Europeans*, a crueller text that the RSC had rejected for the reason Barker now understood lay behind all his failure in the moral climate of his time... it lacked *compassion*... it declined to celebrate humanity as the liberal understands humanity... it was not in any sense critical and, consequently, enlightening... it was, in fact, the first of Barker's *Theatre of Catastrophe*, a tragic form that dismissed morality from the stage, substituting for it a visceral, instinctive emotional energy... Barker knew the moral platitudes of his time as well as anyone and wanted to sting them, to test their vigour, but the theatre was afraid of its own public, as Barker knew... he was surrounded by teachers and did not want to teach... in this alone he re-conceived theatre as a site of the ordeal... in one scene alone Barker challenged the moral lassitude of his era, that in which the aristocrat and victorious general Starhemberg provokes and ridicules the beggars of Vienna... a scene so transgressive that in subsequent productions there were frequent requests for it to be cut out... this scene is followed by the same character's confession of his sexual desire for an abandoned old woman who may or may not be his step-mother... such material violates the law of humanist theatre only so long as it is not placed in a *critical context*... this context Barker declined to put in place, thereby effectively banishing himself. Ireland was perplexed. A humanist himself, he nevertheless possessed an imagination that followed Barker's extreme visions as a hound plunges after a startled hare, longing to satisfy him but alarmed by the alterations of the landscape... Barker wrote later of this sense of gathering hostility... the dog himself now, addressed by himself...

Dog
Curl and imitate my patient attitude
The road in both directions is a void
Pale as if washed
Thin as if ironed
Your abject eye will not meet mine
And I know why:
Our gaze would falter and on its sinking line
Some death would caper:
Dog
If animal could lie I'd encourage you
To bark a white joy at the gathering
Of our antagonists
Instead a fret is drumming your wet chest:
Never this lost says dogbreath
Never this lost:
But we ran over the green rim
Toppling in this tray of flints
Milkless and moonless:
Dog
The time was hissing for our accident

Barker had wanted Jessop to play the maimed protagonist Katrin. She had the intellectual dexterity for the role and had read it in public, opposite Le Prevost as Starhemberg. But Ireland's sense of the relations between stage and audience were rigid – he affirmed over and over again the necessity for the public to love and understand characters if they were to accompany them on such severe journeys. Barker dismissed sympathy as an inhibition, a relic from a type of theatre he needed to emerge from. Instead he emphasised the haunting and hypnotic effect of the text delivered in a certain way, without any attempt at winning or earning sympathy. Barker's ally Charles Lamb would later identify the *challenge* as the significant element of the actors' practice in the Barker text. Taking Baudrillard's Seduction Theory as his starting point, Lamb articulated a method with Barker's texts that dispensed with the Stanislavskian model which for fifty years had dominated the English stage with its crippling insistence on objectives and 'truths', in essence a moral activity incapable of representing the complexity of tragedy in Barker's hands. His favoured actresses – in his own hands as director – lacked the qualities Ireland hoped to find, but gave instead an authority at many removes from naturalism both in body and voice. Barker's whole technique in staging was to eliminate extraneous detail and direct concentration onto the physicality and voice of the performer, to elevate the actor out of conventional realism into a condition that dispensed with identification, making the performer lucent with her difference, a difference born of suffering.

Barker wanted a punishing, uncompromised production of his play but Ireland clung to his values and was applauded for making the intractable material 'work'. Scott provided a sympathetic musical element. Lighting was by Ace McCarron, whose manner on stage and behind it appealed to Barker as much as his skills as a designer. As

Barker came to direct, he leaned heavily on McCarron for practical assistance during the technical rehearsal, where his patient and constructive attitude soothed the anxieties always associated with the moment of realisation. Barker's technical rehearsals proceeded without friction. McCarron could invent an effect of light and then make the lamp from salvaged materials. Barker felt the same mixture of gratitude and amazement at this dexterity that he had known as a child, watching his father repair a broken toy…

12

THE SUCCESS OF *THE EUROPEANS* led to Ireland's departure from The Wrestling School. He was invited to become Artistic Director of the Royal Lyceum, the Edinburgh theatre with which he had been associated in the past. Ireland was a Scot and it represented an emotional and artistic triumph. He assured Barker that the company would find a home in Edinburgh, but it was not to be. Barker visited with *(Uncle) Vanya*. There were no further invitations. He experienced similar frustration when McDiarmid secured the prestigious Almeida Theatre in London. McDiarmid staged two in-house Barker plays, one successful, the other unsuccessful. McDiarmid also hosted The Wrestling School's *(Uncle) Vanya* and *Judith*, but the connection faltered. Both theatres had entirely other objectives than, in what seemed to them an act of *auto-da-fé* in putting their prestige behind Barker's uncompromising project. Nowhere is friendship more constrained by pragmatism than in the theatre. These men had done their best by him. In terms of public recognition, the rewards were few. Critically Barker remained an outsider, and was to become yet more so. They hurried on, in McDiarmid's case to a heady acclaim. Barker quarried deeper still into his personal vision of *the art of theatre*. They sensed perhaps his uncharitable judgement of their enterprise…

13

IRELAND PROPOSED THAT DIRECTORS familiar with Barker's work from the past be invited to replace him, on an ad hoc basis. Barker thought this peculiarly insouciant, since the origins of The Wrestling School lay in a repudiation of their methods. He proposed instead to direct the next work himself, and the very casual structure of the company facilitated this. *Hated Nightfall* was not Barker's first experience of directing actors. He had taken the company to Siena three years previously to the Dionysia Festival, a unique event in which authors from Europe and Africa were invited to direct new plays on their own behalf in the Tuscan countryside. Barker's *Ego In Arcadia* was intended to play outdoors in the evening light, a prospect which suggested numerous possibilities to him… he took with him Melanie Jessop and Tricia Kelly from the *Victory* company, as well as Bill Stewart, an actor for whom Barker had a profound respect and who gave here one of the most outstanding performances Barker had ever seen, plunging from chagrin to self-pity, from whimsy to contempt, simultaneously ugly and beautiful, spiritual and coarse, the apotheosis of contradiction and the ecstasy that is unleashed by it. How few saw it, and how this struck Barker as the authentic nature of great work, which flourishes as a secret, is witnessed as an accident and is extinguished as swiftly as it is seen...

Barker was relieved when poor weather obliged them to perform indoors, in the ancient barn they had rehearsed in. In any case Ireland, flying out late to join them as an actor, had refused point-blank Barker's request that he walk naked into the distant meadows following the death of his character, thinking it churlish. But Barker thought seriously about nakedness in theatre and used it cautiously, with discretion, and never to humiliate. Later it became a powerful element of his stagecraft. Whereas he had planned the set outdoors to be a smouldering bed, he was now required to design a substitute for a long room. Instinctively he seized on the key element of the bed – the sheets – and hung a dozen of them from the rafters, significantly burned... Barker had found directing difficult, even with a group of actors so well-disposed to him as these, for he always wrote blindly, unknowing, and now was called upon to describe, to do what always he found difficult, in private and in public life, namely, to *reveal*... when Ireland, both caring and impatient, substituted himself for Barker in the final week, Barker did not demur. He had, in any case, become exhausted by argument with Ireland over the familiar territory of sympathy and clarity and at this time lacked the

wherewithal – moral or theoretical – to impose his will…
to trust his preference…

14

BARKER SOMETIMES WROTE FOR ACTORS.
Downchild in *Downchild* was conceived for McDiarmid,
as was Dancer in *Hated Nightfall*. He wrote *Judith* for
Jessop, and *Und*. When he knew Wicks, he wrote for her
again and again, describing her, witnessing her on stage,
and describing her again. His favourite actors led him
from one phase to another, a classic instance of mutual
infatuation both in the artistic and the private sphere…

Barker's production of *Hated Nightfall* was tran-
sitional. Whilst he suggested crucial elements of the design
to Engels, he had not yet the confidence to *command* the
design, and besides, Engels was an artist and not a mechanic.
Similarly with *(Uncle) Vanya* whilst Barker proposed the
design to Robin Don, he could not *order* it. He had not yet
grasped – or dared contemplate grasping – the essence of
his method as it later materialised, the totality of his vision
and the necessity to integrate every aspect except one – the
lighting – within his own visual and audial consciousness.
Similarly, Matthew Scott provided the music and sound,
here as for Barker's marionette piece, *All He Fears*. The
power of Barker's own prejudices in the artistic field – and
he trusted the prejudice of artists more than their fragile
logic – would compel him to bring all these aspects under
his own direct control, to become his own designer of set,

costume and sound, as well as writer and director. This absolute authority of the writer lent new meaning to the anaemic concept of 'writers' theatre' and was possible only because The Wrestling School lent Barker full autonomy; and The Wrestling School was itself a unique organisation, operating under its own rules, in effect, without rules. There can have been few more cogent demonstrations of the creative power of the independent ensemble than The Wrestling School under Barker's own direction. Few even of his worst enemies could bring themselves to deny the sheer beauty of the work, however they reviled its methods or its meanings...

Ireland's *Victory* had visited Gennevilliers, Sobel's Brechtian theatre in Paris, and Sobel had misunderstood it, thinking its epic journey Brechtian, but Bradshaw is no Mother Courage and she demonstrates nothing but the tragic fact that things are only what they are... she abolishes any suggestion they might be different...

Now the company had a producer in Neil Wallace and he had the producer's appetite for revelation... he wanted Europe to know Barker... he had invited *The Europeans* to his Glasgow Tramshed and now proposed taking *Hated Nightfall* to the Odéon in Paris. Wallace had superabundant energy, he fumed with his enthusiasms and clashed with Ireland, who himself fumed. Barker watched them smash against each other in their frustration like loose trucks. But Wallace fixed a critical engagement for the company and the Odéon received not one but two of the company's productions, for Ireland had got leave from the Lyceum to direct *The Castle*, a play he admired but in the event lacked the time to properly prepare. The Paris public enthusiastically endorsed *Hated Nightfall* but recoiled from *The Castle*, unable to relate both works to the same author… Barker was dismayed but unsurprised… he had watched Ireland's method with his tragic plays degenerate into apology, such that *The Castle*, a play of appalling passions and bottomless despair, appeared to some as a comedy, stripped of its power in order to accommodate a public that was patronisingly perceived as incapable of tolerating the burden of its pain…

15

BARKER DISLIKED COMPROMISE, and was reluctant to delegate. If theatre is a collaborative art, he brought to it a poet's innate self-reference, and pushed theatre nearer to the poem and the poem nearer to the stage. He was solitary by instinct and was known to few, and those chiefly women. He declared he was made of the women who loved him… but he learned to talk, both in public and to his collaborators, the actors and technicians who were dedicated to his work and willing to adhere to his method. The production of *Judith* represented a massive surge in his personal and artistic confidence, the first occasion on which his *longing*, so routinely suppressed by theatre's division of labour, burst its bonds of silence and decorum, disciplines that suffocated him but which he replaced by a discipline fiercer still, that of a total aesthetic for which he alone assumed responsibility…

Let us describe the first characteristic necessary to the artist who becomes his own *metteur-en-scène*, for the initial conundrum is that he knows too much, if not *everything-that-there-is-to-be-known*, and this is painful because much must inevitably be born again, for if the making of the text was first birth, production is another. The artist – if he *is* an artist – must assume another aspect of himself in order to view his own creation... and we will not pretend this is an *objectivity*, for objectivity is available to no one... Barker came to himself as an artist whose profoundly theatrical imagination operated in the visual as well as the literary sphere... he located his work in its three dimensions; having written it at his desk, he re-imagined it for the stage and, in the case of *Judith*, with unrelenting invention...

Judith was unlike any Wrestling School production that had been seen before and its innovations lay precisely in the area Barker affected to be least interested in, the work's relation with its audience... Barker's argument with Ireland belonged here also, and he had repudiated all devices and techniques designed to assure the audience, to *engage* it, in an off-hand manner, thinking such initiatives diluted the authority of the work. What he now knew was that the audience needed to enter the space of the performance – its darkness, according to Barker, a darkness both real and metaphorical – in a *condition*... this condition had to be different from the condition of other theatres but also from the world outside the theatre. How was this to be achieved? Barker's early enthusiasm for a theatre, a building whose every element led to the experience of the play, could never materialise. He had a profound loathing for the foyer, a space indelibly associated with entertainment and conviviality, a place of gesturing and chatter, the very converse of the sacred vestibule he admired in the old church, a space of silence and preparation for the experience of prayer. Such conditions for the audience's reception of the play could never be replicated in the theatres in which The Wrestling School was invited to play and, indeed, did not exist, the cult of entertainment having annexed the foyer for a dozen functions in all theatres, large or small. Barker was therefore compelled to begin this transformation of the audience *inside* the auditorium by employing the device of a stage-action which began prior to the opening of the doors and ran directly into the performance when the public had settled. There was nothing new in this practice, known in Germany as the *Vorspiel* and by Barker from the Greek *exordium*. The intention was always to draw the audience away from its conviviality and to compel its focus onto the stage, to place it in a new frame of reference, to rinse it of the concerns and triviality of the street, domesticity, friendship or even love, and through the strangeness and volume of the sound and the uncommon image (a repetitive but still complicated routine) to create that condition of *anxiety* that Barker deemed propitious for the reception of his tragedies...

So *Judith* was innovatory in this, and this innovation permitted others, the audience being initiated at the outset, even as they took their seats, into different expectations – or perhaps, having their expectations *removed*, left open to others... Barker had two of his closest allies on the stage, Jessop whom he loved and for whom he had written the title role, and Jane Bertish, who had played his work before The Wrestling School and would remain a significant presence in it. They were joined by William Chubb, who went on to play the anatomist Doja in *He Stumbled* four years later... Barker's exordium had Chubb as Holofernes kneeling at a tin bath in his tent and pouring water over his head, the sound of this activity magnified by a concealed microphone. The tent itself was inside-out, the ropes thereby making a cat's cradle through which the performers weaved their routes. Bertish, in her role as Servant, moved continuously on a plotted path with a feather duster, attentive to a row of suspended busts of the head of Holofernes, her actions and his washed by a surge of sound – a mixture of a haunting, slowed bell and the rattle of rifle bolts. The comprehensive image of the exordium was of military power, imperial authority, and a touching vulnerability located in Chubb's stooping shoulders. All these elements of the exordium were used subsequently... when Judith has committed the murder and the Servant saws off the head, she pours her unwanted gift – a bottle of wine – into the bath, the sound of the liquid in the tub again magnified and a displacement of blood to a place no less chilling to contemplate. The beheading of Holofernes employed a similar technique. Exhausted from her labour of butchery, Bertish climbed off the floor and with household scissors snipped the twine that held one of the several busts of the dead captain, catching it in a bag... in all these stage actions, Barker threw off with infinite pleasure the conventions of naturalism which he thought suffocated theatre, and substituted intensely conceived imagery that sustained the emotional pressure of the performance and the text, without risking the peculiar bathos of mimesis and its attendant deflation... (*'how did they cut off his head...?'* Always theatre's weakness lay in the fallacies of even the most brilliantly achieved realistic effects...)

Judith's design was by Robert Innes Hopkins, exquisitely realising Barker's decisions, including the setting of the costume in the 19th century, thus abolishing the picturesque representations of biblical times and simultaneously deepening the obligation on the audience to permit the *inauthentic* into its experience...

16

BARKER'S NEXT PRODUCTION, his rewritten Chekhov, *(Uncle) Vanya*, employed Robin Don to realise Barker's rusting freighter with its rising flights of iron stairs, the last time he would work alongside a stage designer. From *Ursula* onwards he made his own designs under the name Tomas Leipzig, employing a technical assistant to draw up plans and communicate with workshops... similarly, his costume designs were credited to the imaginary Billy Kaiser... Barker knew well the English prejudice against writers directing their own works... he did not wish to compound his offence by admitting he was entirely responsible for every visual and audial element as well... these fictional friends, with their international credentials, earned excellent reviews for their beautiful and austere framing of Barker's texts which, by contrast, routinely attracted bad notices...

Barker's antipathy for Chekhov lay only partly in their contrasting artistic personalities... rather, he was critical of the theatre's annexation and exploitation of Chekhov to pander to what he felt was a climate of self-disgust and spiritual defeatism... as a tragic author Barker believed the experience of tragedy lent power to its public precisely through its revelation of pain, its intimacy with death... he repudiated any notion that Chekhov could be counted as a tragic writer and thought the melancholy of the Chekhovian text – its celebration of failure and impotence – contributed to a collective denial of possibility, a tasteful closure, even a state of torpor which was the converse of that creative anxiety Barker sought from his own stage works... for him Chekhov's huge authority in English theatre was a symptom of a spiritual malaise, all the more infectious for being seductive... in eviscerating *Uncle Vanya* to make his own *(Uncle) Vanya* (the parenthesised domestic title being the merest suggestion of the protagonist's struggle to cast off the patronising manner of his circle and to reclaim his full name, Ivan, and the dignity that goes with it) Barker ran headlong into unanimous critical contempt, as he fully expected to. His argument about the political and sociological use made of classic texts, fully articulated in programme notes, was addressed by nobody. The critical establishment at this point chose not to engage with Barker and would never do so again. For the subsequent period, his work went largely unreviewed and, consequently, unadvertised. Barker and The Wrestling School could continue to exist only by the dedication of the ensemble, whose reward as performers came only from the performance itself. Indeed there was ample evidence that actors who consistently played for the company handicapped themselves elsewhere in their careers, and certain theatre agents actively dissuaded their clients from joining the ensemble. A fragile structure – a tent of sticks – sustained the company's public identity. Its following was loyal, and Barker's own reputation in drama teaching, combined with the dedicated scholarship of Barker exponents like David Ian Rabey and Charles Lamb, ensured a student contingent made up a substantial part of its public. But those theatres whose artistic directors believed in Barker were few and had little to gain from admitting him. The Wrestling School became a *rumour*, its very existence a denial of the laws of entertainment, its appearances unadvertised, so that it came and went unnoticed except by the cognoscenti or those who, by accident or by secret signs, had found their way to it and emerged amazed... Barker stated in an interview for a Paris magazine that 'he did not know the theatre and the theatre did not know him...' a rhetorical flourish that contained a withering truth. Barker preferred it that way, and Corner struggled with the consequences...

17

MELANIE JESSOP HAD PLAYED HELENA in a public reading of *(Uncle) Vanya*, again opposite Nicholas Le Prevost, as she had in *The Europeans*, but again she was not to create the role in the full production. Her affair with Barker had been tempestuous, simultaneously creative and agonising. She chose to put an end to it rather than endure the ordeal of playing a role so replete with the erotic values Barker's writing characterised. Barker and his assistant Sarah Le Brocque could not discover a suitable replacement. The audition for Barker was a moment of revelation, also of definition. He knew at once, by intuition, when the right actor had appeared, and the actor, in turn, manifested the role almost prior to rehearsal. This quality of recognition – as if the character and the performer were one, but had walked the streets in ignorance of one another prior to the event – occurred frequently but not invariably in Barker's practice. In desperation he had appealed for more leading actresses to interview. He required in Helena a physical dignity, a capacity for movement on the stage, both light and assured, and a dexterity with speech that he came to realise – and he was not alone in this – was becoming scarce as the drama schools failed in their obligations to keep voice at the heart of their teaching. The disease of naturalism, as Barker characterised it, combined with the increasingly dominant part played by television in the culture, and *its* wholesale capitulation to naturalism, ensured that the training of young actors prioritised 'realism' and minimised the disciplines of projection and articulation, both of which were in any case politically suspect in a regime that denigrated all manifestations of 'elitism', whether in dress or speech. Barker made no secret of his belief – scarcely a *credo*, only a statement of self-evident facts – that elitism in art was inevitable, as the fact that night follows day

– self-selecting groups would always line up behind new forms which appalled the majority, at least until they in turn became *conventions*. His whole experience supported this. He argued for – and demanded of his actors – a clarity in delivery that was best served by the standard spoken English known as 'received pronunciation', because the density of his texts, in order to be followed by a public less and less familiar with complexity, required the most direct transmission. Accents – regional or national – even a highly personalised style of playing the role – inhibited this. Barker's style as director followed his style as writer. The more depth and contradiction contained within the speech, the more essential became a distinctive mode of delivery. In auditioning Victoria Wicks, Barker came simultaneously to a threshold in his personal and artistic life.

18

WICKS CAME WITH A REPUTATION but Barker knew nothing of it. He rarely watched television and she was the star of an award-winning television comedy which ran to five series… devotees haunted the stage door long after its demise, but she paid it scant attention and did not include it in her programme-biography for many years. Her manner in audition was startlingly simple and she asked few questions. She wore no make-up nor was she dressed either to reveal her figure or to imply her suitability for the role, as an actress might, and legitimately… She spoke quietly, and her demeanour was modest, though not because she was afraid. Barker was gracious with actors and neither condescended nor required to overawe... if theatre had turned his shyness into a weight of stone, his assumption of the director's role, once he embraced it, relieved him. He had never lacked faith in himself but now he found himself comfortable in his own authority. The tent of sticks was adequate shelter... after Wicks's departure Barker turned to his assistant Sarah Le Brocque and invited her opinion... they were unanimous that at the last moment they had found the actress for the role. If the rehearsal was ruptured at the end of its first week by the decision of Hugh Fraser not to proceed to play Vanya (a crisis resolved by his replacement with William Armstrong, an actor whose neurotic energy stimulated the company), Wicks's presence and concentration were a calming influence, now and in subsequent productions. Whilst Barker had been impressed by her demeanour and vocal range, he could not have predicted the invention Wicks brought to her stage actions, nor her recklessness in persisting with them, no matter what the risk to herself... in leaping onto a fragile chair to study herself in a great mirror like a zoo animal, she showed a febrile dexterity wholly in keeping with Helena's neurotic self-regard... but her lightness of foot, sense of balance and sheer grace were never seen to better advantage than in her entrance from the beach where Astrov has waylaid and raped Helena... Barker's exordium in *(Uncle) Vanya* consisted of a choreographed passage of household servants over high iron staircases to the sound of a repeated fraction of Bartok's 4th String Quartet... this routinely punctuated by the dropping of tin crockery and trays onto the steel floor below, a fractious and unnerving racket that causes the sleeping Astrov to jerk out of sleep over and over again and the audience to sense the wholly un-Chekhovian nature of the ordeal that awaits them... this debris created an unstable floor of sliding metal, often jagged from the drops and never silent, never still... Barker indicated that Wicks should enter from the beach, stage left, but walking backwards, a sign of her distress, but understood in the technical rehearsal that if it was a dilemma for all the actors to manoeuvre on the treacherous floor, it would be particularly perilous for her, barefoot and wearing a slip, an invitation to cruel accidents... Wicks knew the value of the spectacle and persevered in what was to be one of the most memorable entrances in theatre... if Barker had made a menacing chaos of the stage, Wicks seized the opportunity to intensify Helena's pain by staggering backwards on the clattering trays, always teetering on the edge of a wounding fall, always delivering the audience into a state of apprehension and never once taking a fall... it was for Barker a revelation of the actor as unearthly in her capacity for risk, both moral and physical... few would have done it and Wicks was not yet his lover... when later she played naked on stage she declared it was for love, but here it was pure inspiration and the outcome of a faith in the text and the man who had made it... Barker's American ally, the director Richard Romagnoli, thought Wicks achieved a transcendent spirituality he had never witnessed on stage and at the curtain call ran from one side of the empty circle to the other, two fingers in his mouth and whistling his encouragement to a usually stagnant and unresponsive audience, few in number and somehow *hurt*…

19

BARKER'S ENCOUNTER WITH WICKS came as a revelation… he had worked with actresses of greater reputation… none possessed her physical dexterity, her elegance or her self-sacrificing tragic *manner*, for Barker now knew and demanded the price of tragic performance and saw how few were able to give it. He wrote again and again both for her body and her voice, and the two were in her an unfaltering symbiosis. He warned her – unnecessarily because she knew it by intuition – that in playing his roles she would never be loved by a public, because the public could never pity her, and in any case tragedy dispensed with pity and achieved its effects by other means. No audience would ever identify with the roles played by Victoria Wicks, but identification was a blind alley, and her admirers talked instead of her inspiration, itself an element of her bravery. She abolished sentimentality from her performance, she coaxed nothing from her public but dared it to admire her through the outrage it felt at what it was she said… the ecstasy she carried in her performance was entirely appropriate to the content of Barker's speeches… she perhaps played defiance and sexuality in combination more powerfully than any actress of the time… for all that he had enemies in profusion among the critical establishment, Barker knew in her nothing would be sacrificed to expediency or ever modified for the sake of comforting an uneasy house…

20

WALLACE GOT *(UNCLE) VANYA* to Berlin, as he had got *Judith* to Amsterdam, and he suffered their failure personally. Many who had come to Barker as if torch-bearers for his genius experienced the identical shame and crept away embarrassed by the association. In the Hebbel foyer a silence made of iron had fallen over the canapés. Barker, emerging from the auditorium, stood alone, unadorned by the management who had invited him but who now, with Wallace, were stricken with that shifty demeanour known only to the doyens of theatre, men and women pitifully susceptible to public disdain. Did Barker ever grow accustomed to it? What unhealthy growth of scales does an artist require to smother him if he is not to suffer this humiliation – not of public hostility, which he predicts, but of the frigidity of his so-called friends? This it was his fate to suffer, but never the denial of the performers, who are anyway disinclined to shame, hardly knowing what it is… they came from their dressing-rooms and ushered him away into the Berlin night…

Barker saw the confidence draining from Wallace but immediately proposed *Ursula* as the next production… he had seen his way with the legend from a painting by Cranach, an altar-piece in Dresden, and he had two actors he now felt compelled to play on stage in a vortex of desire, Wicks and O'Callaghan... O'Callaghan had the profile and the sexual pride of a Renaissance ruler and Barker made him the Prince of the Estuary, betrothed to Ursula but overwhelmed by Placida, a convent superior discovering her sexuality and prepared to murder for it... Wallace reluctantly agreed but already he was thinking if the company was to survive it required name-actors and plays of proven popularity, like *Scenes*... Barker opened *Ursula* on the main stage of Birmingham Rep knowing the theatre expected it to fail and untroubled by it... he was secure within his own allegiances... Wicks, Callaghan and Claire Price provided a dynamic centre... McCarron gave the stage the austere but exquisite light that refined the monochromatic style of the company... Barker as Leipzig designed a set of steel and flying photography... Lucy Weller interpreted his needs in costume, the last time before Billy Kaiser assumed full responsibility for costume, and the choreography of the eleven virgins was by Sue Nash. Matthew Scott, uncomfortable with the new order of The Wrestling School, worked with the chorus, but Barker's integrated style now made a composer unnecessary and Barker himself designed the soundscape from fractional elements of Ligeti, Stockhausen, Berio, Jani Cristou, Bartok and Bach... the abstract sounds of Barker's productions, which entailed a large number of cues, along with the exordium, became recognisable characteristics of his style... inside this framework of aesthetic values he was simultaneously evolving a theory of performance, made necessary by the growing complexity of his texts and the poetic character of them...

Ursula was a respectable success in Birmingham to the evident chagrin of *the dramaturgy*... it challenged the conventional wisdom that theatre had a responsibility to address issues of contemporary 'relevance'... a concept Barker found patronising of the public and profoundly destructive of the nature of theatre experience... when *Ursula* was nominated by public ballot for the TMA Theatre Awards (Best New Play), a significant conflict was implicitly revealed, one Barker had identified in his own theoretical works, such as *Arguments For A Theatre*... for the other nominated play was a work of extreme contemporaneity, naturalistic, and was directed by Birmingham's artistic director William Alexander, who had directed Barker's early plays for the RSC. In the event, Alexander's play took the prize, but significantly at this stage of the competition, the public's judgement was eliminated in favour of the decision of a committee of critics. The outcome was therefore never in doubt, and Barker anyway took a mischievous pleasure in having never won any of the prestigious awards of the English theatre in his entire career... the result nevertheless confirmed the political nature of a theatre system with which Barker was increasingly in conflict...

Ursula did not visit Berlin but played to full houses in Copenhagen... Denmark was generous to Barker and had applauded *(Uncle) Vanya* when it played in a reduced version in an old packing plant on the waterfront... Barker thought Denmark's supreme civility enabled tragedy to be experienced there in a way that a disturbed, neurotic society like England, with its obsessive appetite for comedy, could not... he directed Danish actors in *Wounds*

To The Face some years later, but could not achieve what he required from them... the Danish public enthusiastically endorsed The Wrestling School and particularly identified the vocal quality of Wicks as being peculiarly un-English in its range and depth... her physical dexterity had been fully exercised in *Ursula* as it was to be in every production of the ensemble, and Barker did not hesitate to advertise her sexuality on stage... on her side she dissented from none of his decisions and was in this way exemplary for the entire acting company... that they were lovers, everybody knew; as they also knew this disposed her personally to endorse his method and his intention, but she was scrupulous in demanding nothing from him or the production that was not available to others, took less time than some in rehearsal, and gave herself without reservation to the needs of the play. When she came to perform in *Gertrude – The Cry* she was 45 years old. Few actresses would contemplate such exposure in speech and body that Barker asked of her. That she triumphantly exemplified the bravery both of the character and the performer was testament to the power of the text – a text he could never have written without her – but also to the power of their passion. Wicks led Barker's imagination and he, in turn, re-imagined her and in so doing refined his own attitude to theatre. The relationship was not in any sense domestic – Wicks was married with a child, Barker in a long, profoundly intimate relationship with the art historian Marcia Pointon, a liaison cruelly and swiftly ended by the poignant exposure of *Gertrude – The Cry*...

21

BARKER'S MONOLOGUE for one actress *Und* was seized on by Wallace as the perfect text to inveigle a *star performer* into The Wrestling School and thereby lift it from its tenuous and obscure position. Wallace was nothing if not a realist in theatre and knew if things were to thrive they must expand... he had attended business training courses and spoke the language of *growth*, he believed in laws of *development* and wanted The Wrestling School to discover a *system*... Barker thought there might be a system also, but not that proposed by Wallace... When Wallace intimated that Juliet Stevenson might accept *Und*, Barker was unwilling... he admired Stevenson and she had played Barker in Los Angeles and was to play him on radio, but he had written the part for Melanie Jessop and he was dogged in his loyalties, he could not have understood the principle of an ensemble that replaced actresses for reasons of expediency... to *draw attention*... he wanted the work to *command* attention in itself... and in any case he distrusted an audience that came for a performer, he thought it a distortion of theatre even if for many it was the substance of it... Barker was increasingly certain that his theatre had to find its *raison d'être* in some other place, in some different motivation, that the experience of tragedy needed to know itself as a *need* and not a thing to which a public had to be *persuaded* by a string of *attractions*... so he insisted on keeping faith with himself, and Jessop took the role of Und, a solitary Jewess waiting impatiently for her own extinction... *Und* was supremely unnaturalistic and Jessop a non-naturalistic performer... her personal beauty had fascinated Barker on her first audition for *Victory* years before... they were no longer emotionally involved but their communication was such that rehearsal was painless, a permanent development to the moment of performance. Jessop had high status as a performer and shared Barker's contempt for petty seductive techniques. In a ball-gown of white plastic, dazzling to the eye, she exclaimed, bewailed, soared and collapsed on a set of a mechanical lethality designed by Barker/Leipzig with the indispensable assistance of Ace McCarron... a dozen trays loaded with significant objects flew into the performance space on steel rods at intervals during Und's decline... the floor smoked... water cascaded from above... for more than an hour Jessop sustained an ordeal that tested her and her public and made *Und* almost the definitive play of Barker's tragic theory, an unrelenting volume of energy and pain that begged to be repudiated for its excess but demanded simultaneously that excess be accommodated... theatre here for Barker was theatre because it could be *nothing else*... it could never be subsumed into another form... not film... not television... every element demanded not only the live performance but the *sacrifice* of the performer...

22

BARKER'S CONVICTION that the theatre never asked enough of its public and that the public was in turn corrupted by its lack of ambition justified his method to himself but Wallace was nearly out of patience and Corner was struggling to book the tour without which the company could not exist... having got his way with *Ursula* and *Und* Barker thought it politic to submit... Wallace made contact with leading actresses who might consent to play Galactia, the stubborn painter-heroine of *Scenes From An Execution*, a play of impeccable humanitarian, pacifist values that Barker himself could no longer entertain but which was now a classic of the European theatre if typically unknown in his own country since McDiarmid's Almeida premiere... Kathryn Hunter joined, drawn by a role for which she felt considerable personal sympathy (as had the future socialist politician Glenda Jackson, and all those actresses who had performed it, including Juliet Stevenson...). Barker was at odds with himself and with his own text. On the level of the dramaturgical content, he was frustrated by the character's moral earnestness, a moral earnestness that he had come to dislike in all human beings but found particularly irksome in theatre where he now thought the protagonist required to challenge the audience with her ostensible *lack* of sympathy... he could not discover a means of drawing the audience and the stage into a conflict, a *creative anxiety* that had to be the essence of tragic experience... *Scenes* was by no means a tragedy but his method was inflexible and Hunter could not play tragedy, her own instincts as a performer were to make a bond between the character and the public, a thing all-too-easy to do for her and for the character... Barker remained a mystery to Hunter and the play's ending – the 'yes' with which Galactia accords the state its patronage over her talent – troubled her as it had troubled Jackson. Barker said Galactia was spent, exhausted, and would never paint again, but Hunter found this barely tolerable... the fact was that Barker had only limited sympathy with artists and knew their intrinsic corruptibility, a thing non-artists with a pitiful longing for faith prefer never to contemplate... Barker's production stressed Galactia's selfishness, her ruthless exploitation of others, and strained to make the arguments of her enemies more cogent – he hated the idea that the moral power might rest with Galactia and disliked actors bringing their political prejudices onto the stage – but Hunter could not find it in herself to collaborate in what she perhaps dimly suspected was a self-destructive enterprise... the production was nevertheless entirely within the aesthetic Barker had created and fluent, using a massive wooden crate as the playing area, the surface of which, by means of trapdoors, delivered props or furniture. The exordium was the nearest yet to a situationist work of art, having three disabled sailors crying out in wheelchairs, and a sail plunging into a steel tank from which it emerged, dripping with the sea water that is the environment of the painting that gives the play its title...

23

SCENES GRATIFIED WALLACE and depressed Barker in equal quantities... both were instructed... Wallace was obliged to recognise that new works always had a greater fascination for the public than revivals, whether or not these revivals were classics in Barker's oeuvre (and there had been talk of a new *Love Of A Good Man* as well...), and Barker's own attitude towards the direction of actors was informed by what he had recognised in Hunter's performance and had failed to eliminate...

For all that Wallace was compelled to admit that Barker had now delivered three superlative productions (*Ursula*, *Und* and *Scenes*...), the producer in him was frustrated at the lack of visible *progress* (a concept Barker had long ago forsaken...) and he had taken a powerful post in Haarlem as director of a three-stage theatre, which – in conformity with the experience of Ireland and McDiarmid – signally failed to offer The Wrestling School accommodation... critically, a *cordon sanitaire* was now in place around Barker and where his work was not reviled it was ignored... in certain cases (the prestigious critic Martin Esslin...) there was a permanent propaganda of hostility which damaged his reputation... in others the sheer scale of the malice and incomprehension rendered the reviewers comic, and their reviews were quoted in academic circles as samples of critical *grostesquerie* (Lyn Gardner) ...as a counterweight to this, Barker's standing in Europe was high and in France he earned the support of superlative translators and publishers, as well as directors who returned again and again to stage his works... Barker knew that as far as his own country was concerned the hostility of the establishment would be a dirge forever sounding in his ears... he was clever and stood accused of cleverness... charged with stubbornness, he repudiated whatever aptitude for compromise he ever possessed... few artists could have persisted in these conditions... whereas The Wrestling School gave him unique prestige and opportunity (it was the only state-funded theatre company established around a single dramatist) its existence, and Barker's own authoritative style as its director, militated against other theatres ever mounting his plays (Colchester's Mercury Theatre was an honourable exception and mounted *The Europeans* in a production by Janice Dunn) ...and many of his works were premiered in foreign countries... Barker thought the National Theatre a sordid institution for the simple reason that it could only ever reproduce the national ideology... its incumbent directors would always be selected for their readiness to endorse it and in every regard it would be politically and spiritually incapable of mounting his plays... the successive regimes of Hall, Eyre, Nunn and Hytner amply demonstrated this... they and their *dramaturgy* (Barker consciously misappropriated the word, making a collective noun out of a function... he thought the professional dramaturgs an obstacle to significant movement in theatre) entertained a spectrum of writers as if to demonstrate their catholicity of taste, but their political prejudice and its aesthetic consequences could only have one outcome... a superficial critique of society lingered in or even dominated most of the productions... in few cases did it ever seriously threaten the entertainment value of the *product*... and for such institutions art was necessarily a product, conditioned by accountancy and pre-eminently *for sale*... Barker had amused himself by notoriously sending the National Theatre all his plays for a certain period... and he would not have refused their performance if offers had been made, for he was not averse to a range of styles of playing his texts being put before a public even if he thought those styles less potent than his own and the institutions dishonest... he knew the artist must bid farewell to his work... his concern was to establish the values that underlay a modern tragedy and to demonstrate them in the first instance with The Wrestling School... thereafter he knew full well he might never recognise his texts again...

24

BARKER REJOICED IN THE DEPARTURE of Wallace, finding his influence burdensome... he hated all forms of supervision, even that which came bearing dreams or promises... if *Ursula* had shown Barker's flair for directing in the largest spaces, he now welcomed the inevitable retreat into studios, certain he could operate more fluently the fewer criteria he was obliged to satisfy... the Barker/Leipzig sets for *He Stumbled*, *A House Of Correction*, *Gertrude – The Cry*, *13 Objects* and *Dead Hands* exemplified his intentions to create acting environments that repudiated all compromise with naturalism and turned the studio spaces – routinely condemned to housing naturalistic domestic interiors – into startling, active settings for voice and movement... The Wrestling School was identified with a visual and sonic style as much as with a text that overwhelmed and violated the confined spaces in which it was imprisoned... this was entirely Barker's intention... he believed in plethora... he had contempt for narrow enlightenment projects in theatre… his loud exordia were calls to new ways with theatre that made redundant all conventional expectations of *understanding, sympathy* or *recognition*…

Barker thought style was the outcome of discipline both moral and practical… the more certain it became, the more it reflected a severe intellectual attitude which was critical not of society itself but of the moral platitudes that corrupted it and in turn corrupted theatre, turning it into a register of *opinion*… he thought tragedy dispensed with hope, was 'hope-less', which was its power… in creating catastrophic situations his plays evaded the suffocating moral criteria that attach to conventional realism… always he strove to lever his actors and his public out of the territory of the familiar to which they are attracted as flies are witlessly drawn to rotting meat… he did not want his audience to become more *critical* – the aim of the dominant theatre of his time, and no longer an ambition but a *habit* – he wanted it drawn into an ecstasy by the spectacle of excess even to the *contemplation of death* which is the essence of tragedy…

25

BARKER'S SEXUALITY DOMINATED his theatre and his life…

In the dark I tripped her
I got her down on stones

Oceans from conversations
Cities from goodwill
The stars ganged thickly on a branch
They knew I'd kill for her mouth
For all her mouths I'd kill
Wife of agility her thigh goes
Higher than advertisements

It rescued him from despair and simultaneously provided him with an emotional and speculative territory for his art... he knew there was a politics of sexual love and tried to define it... in his own life he had suffered and luxuriated in the collisions of desire and could not rid himself of the idea the collisions were necessary, integral to ecstasy... he had a dread of the closure of love whilst knowing its innate compulsion to closure...

The husband
Have I misunderstood
Goes into the sheets a prisoner:
So give him the bread of your belly
Give him the water of your breasts
I see your lips drift
And the slow rise of your legs
It is the same
Why disguise the sameness from myself?

The relationship of the director to his leading actress is always a subject for speculation, curiosity and not infrequently malevolence... few dramatists have not been lovers of actresses... some of these passions have been legendary, none induced a more extensive body of work than Barker's for Wicks... she sacrificed her career as a television actress for him, at least in the opinion of many... her agents abandoned her, unable to tolerate a client who earned neither money nor acclaim, for they are soulless hirers in the main... and Wicks, along with the ensemble as a whole, was rarely applauded, the single element of all that hostile criticism that wounded and embittered him, for in their rage against him the critics disdained to notice the passion of the actors...

She appeared naked in *Gertrude – The Cry* and in *The Fence In Its Thousandth Year*, she was unclothed in *The Ecstatic Bible*, in *13 Objects*, in *Animaux En Paradis*... but just as Barker's way with language derogated naturalism, so in his staging of the sexual, he believed a greater power lay in the uncompleted, the stopped or the unreal... Barker thought all killing and all sex beyond the possibility of adequate representation in the theatre space – it was an ethical not a mimetic problem... thus in the sexual encounters of Gertrude and Claudius Barker eschewed a conventional representation of the act and relied for effect upon the startling image of the actress naked but for her shoes, taken standing from behind, all this accompanied by the harsh discordances of Ligeti edited and looped... this in itself could never be enough for Barker's intense emotional investment in the writing and staging of sexual desire... as the poisoned king awakes from his sleep – an awakening to death – he sees before his eyes the preposterous act of sex performed by his murderers and emits a final and appalling howl which coincides with their cry of desperate love… a cacophony of human extremity that surely must be judged the pinnacle of Barker's stagecraft…

Barker's dependence on Wicks at such critical junctures was absolute… the possibility of a withering bathos always lay embedded in such scenes, but she moved like a dancer and wore clothing better than a model… her balance was so fine that she was able, in the same play, to perform the act of a woman recently delivered of a child dressing in high-heeled shoes, standing on one to slip on the other… never did she stumble or falter… but the demands he made on her lay as much in what he caused her to say as in the actions she so skilfully demonstrated, words which, spoken in nakedness, might lacerate an actress… Wicks steeled herself to the ordeal of the performance, sustained by an absolute faith in the work and her love for its creator, but the tension came through and had to come through… this sense of danger in all she did was implicit in the writing… not only was she-the-actress and she-the-character drawn into terrible territory, but the audience was simultaneously exposed… it was an anxiety that Barker believed to be religious in its essence… a revelation of unspoken life articulated in the darkness of a room where neither legality nor morality had a place except in their upheaval…

She enabled him… she was critical in the making of the equation and she was the obsessive subject of his regard… conventional moral criticism, whether from conservatives or feminists, could not dispose of the aesthetic erotic power of his staging and her bravery in realising it, for criticism insinuates itself at the points of weakness and she allowed none… in *13 Objects* she flung up her skirts to be thrashed by a vagrant over a drum… in *The Fence In Its Thousandth Year* she manoeuvred backwards to a frontier fence to fling up her expensive skirts and copulate with scarcely visible strangers… she denied Barker nothing in imagination and the confidence of her playing lent him further courage to dream… Wicks knew she was never degraded by him but that his skills in direction would always create beauty from her pain… in the deep, womanly tones of her voice his text was safe from violation… in the litheness of her body his imagery was lent that element of the *uncanny* Barker sought on the stage, for he thought in their extremity actors were scarcely human…

> *Her arse:*
> *And doors slammed on uncompleted sentences:*
> *The oaths of all the world's mad mothers*
> *Could not recall the animal that shot from*
> *Under him*
> *Nor comrades flog it to obedience with*
> *Strung bundles of advice:*
> *It raced to where her skirt sang to the*
> *Drumtap of her stride and dogged her:*
> *An estate burned in his eyes*
> *That long seasons of love had cultivated*
> *But he would never be returned:*
> *His brain drowned gratefully…*

Barker's long love affair with Marcia Pointon ended with the performance of *Gertrude – The Cry*, a meditation on the extremes of sexual desire that Wicks had inspired and which uttered through art what could barely be confessed in life. Pointon had been with him in Venice when he saw the painting that inspired *Scenes* and in Visegrad when he saw the castle that inspired *The Castle*. He had written a testament to their love in the long poem *The Ascent Of Monte Grappa* and now he violated his own admonitions…

We have made the ascent and descent
We have stood on the peak breathless with
Incredulity
And now must learn to love the low

Shortly after, Wicks parted from her husband…

26

IN HIS POEMS Barker contemplated the pleasures of ceasing the struggle of a creative life… the sour satisfactions of abject surrender…

To lie exquisitely thwarted

He knew artists who drank heavily and indulged their contempt for the world… he had never much liked the world himself and his character had been shaped by an instinctive dread of the collective… school had been purgatory to him… he shared the prejudices of Horace

Odi profanum vulgus et arceo…

Barker's favourite philosopher Adorno mocked Horace for his snobbery but Barker knew Horace was a slave's son, Adorno a rich man's heir... one knew the people, the other patronised them... yet after twenty years Adorno's book hung out of its covers, loose-leaved, from Barker's studying... he read few plays and his loved poets were never English... Apollinaire... Rilke... Attila József... Paul Celan... and he discovered in Bartok a manner that defined in music his own with the stage... restlessness... incessant invention... as if the world could be understood only through its incongruities... and in a work like *Wounds To The Face* he reproduced the form of the string quartet, themes discarded and recovered, developed, turned against themselves...

27

IF THE ENSEMBLE HAD BEEN EXEMPLARY in *He Stumbled*, and the play's exordium a manifest triumph, with its invitation to the violation of cruel secrets, Barker had cause to yearn for its absence in *A House Of Correction*... he could not assemble his loved company... obliged to audition, he made errors of choice and in a matter of days a sullen atmosphere had settled over the rehearsal... without the presence of two actresses Barker knew and admired, Julia Tarnoky and Jules Melvin, staunch allies from *Ursula*, *The Ecstatic Bible* and *He Stumbled*, he knew he could only have collapsed... the experience was cruel and instructive... three actors of proven ability and cast in the dominant roles were resistant to his method... their training and experience rendered them wholly unsuitable to play Barker and he could not win their allegiance... he urged them to put their faith in the text, to respect the rhythms of the text, to excavate the text and only the text for their characters, but they had been tutored by the heirs of Stanislavsky, they played everything around the text, they clamoured for histories and narratives which might connect them to the world, but the play was situated precisely where the world ceased to be represented... the bad health of the rehearsal sickened the performance itself... the futile and now abandoned search for 'truth...' – a concept Barker repudiated as an obstacle in rehearsal – had stripped these actors of their confidence... one never succeeded in delivering his lines... the others faltered, which cost the production that quality of bravura delivery so critical to Barker's method... his actors *had* to obey the musical law of the text... even the exordium, properly conceived as a surrealist *invitation* to the audience, created a neurotic self-consciousness in the performers, such that one complained of the *loudness* of the soundscape... Barker was injured by the experience but he knew he had taken on the dominant tradition through The Wrestling School and also that his project could be undermined from any direction... on this occasion he had admitted his opponents himself, but it was a general truth that many actors were simply unable to disinvest themselves of the habits of naturalism, and their reluctance to embrace a muscular, poetic and remorseless text, however immersed in imagery, merely reflected the poverty of text-writing, not least in places which declared the text sacred... none of Barker's ensemble had careers originating in the Royal

Court Theatre or under the aegis of its directors, all of whom, in Barker's opinion, had wreaked traumatic injury on the autonomy of the writer in pursuit of a chimerical ideology... that of *social relevance*...

28

IN CONTRAST TO *A House Of Correction*, Barker's ambitions for *Gertrude – The Cry* were fully realised... the acting company included Wicks, O'Callaghan and Bertish, Wicks and O'Callaghan playing the erotic partnership first staged in *Ursula* and Bertish in her finest form as the king's mother, Isola... Barker was frustrated in his casting of Cascan, Gertrude's devoted servant... he had wanted Gerard McArthur, an actor of translucent religiosity who had played the leading role in his eight-hour long epic *The Ecstatic Bible* in Adelaide... but McArthur prevaricated, failing to grasp the centrality of the role which was the highest development yet of Barker's fascination with the servant as a type of semi-religious vocation... he had begun it in *Ten Dilemmas*, developed it in *The Brilliance Of The Servant*, and was to take it on again in *The Fence In Its Thousandth Year*... moreover, McArthur and Wicks had been immaculately cast against one another in Adelaide and Barker believed in acting partnerships... McArthur later regretted his decision but Barker found in Jason Morrell a superb replacement whose powers of service and devotion came from a different place... to these Barker added actors new to him but able to realise both the roles and the spirit of the work… Tom Burke's Hamlet was tender, menacing and coldly philosophical all at the same time, and Justin Avoth, the queen's adolescent lover, became a favourite actor of Barker's, serving him dazzlingly in both *13 Objects* and *Dead Hands*…

Barker's Danish connection ensured a suitable location for its opening, the annual Shakespeare festival in Elsinore Castle… a vapid, musicalised *Hamlet* played in the courtyard below, with a multinational cast and oily pink lighting… the contrast with *Gertrude – The Cry* could hardly have been greater, though the festival had predictably chosen to focus its publicity on the bigger event… this left Barker and The Wrestling School with a rectangular ballroom and no set, with one day to prepare before the opening… these were the conditions in which he thrived… always his decisions were swift, whether in making substitutions or simply throwing away cherished elements of his staging… it was the apotheosis of the writer/designer/director in Barker… but equally, the triumph of a company so confident of itself, so trusting of both him and the material, that they had always been able to stage a performance in almost any situation… they had rehearsed in London for a studio theatre… now all their moves had to be altered to accommodate a baroque hall… Barker had asked for a low platform running its entire length, simply uplit from the floor… the audience were seated on either side… this made perspectives extreme but it was precisely in this distance that Barker achieved his best effects… always he wanted the longest possible entrances and they could never be longer than this… what was more, the audience were now slightly *beneath* the actors and this reversed the normal status-relations between public and stage, something Barker deemed essential for the fullest realisation of tragedy... he made swift and entirely appropriate decisions where the absence of the set posed problems... the most striking being the delivery of the drowned baby to Claudius's feet in the penultimate scene... instead of the child being launched onto the stage on the end of a cable, which then swung to and fro with the menace of a pendulum under Claudius's horrified gaze, Barker had Tom Burke rush the length of the platform with the pitiful bundle on the end of a rope, so it dragged behind him and was abandoned in a startling and disconcerting image that began – such was the length of the stage – some moments before the previous scene had concluded... arguably the Elsinore staging was the most perfect, for its situation in a non-theatre space delivered that sense of incongruity and anxiety that Barker asserted was a prerequisite of tragic experience... for him the purpose-built theatre, with its bars, foyers, safety regulations and upholstered furniture only emphasised what Barker so passionately repudiated – *domesticity*...

29

BARKER SLEPT IN A ROOM with 15 doors... a Japanese visitor, the critic Goro Minamoto, asked if it discomforted him that when he woke he might not know which one to use...? It was the same with his plays... they had many doors by which both to enter and leave... each might be a way to a meaning, for tragedy in his hands never possessed a single interpretation, if *interpretation* could ever be attempted with such complexity... in Barker's small but secret garden, the critic observed here also was a profusion of paths, such that a single object, a chair or urn, might be approached from a number of directions... this was the outcome but Barker never made his garden to a plan, as he never wrote a play knowing its journey or possessing an *intention*... by his method, which was scarcely methodical at all, he allowed his characters an autonomy that abolished any possibility of political or social objectives... the consequence was that any morality – either his characters' or his own – was put at hazard whenever he wrote and this hazarding he believed was an artist's solitary *obligation*...

30

BARKER'S *DEAD HANDS* was the reprise of a theme that underlay much of his mature work... the issue of free will... history's power over the individual... whether history could be evaded by a self-conscious act of anti-history, and in this instance how a man comes into the inheritance of his instincts as well as his property... it was also a further instalment of his investment in the subjects of sexual conspiracy... trespass... and flagrant eroticism... all articulated with that combination of flair and dread that characterised Avoth's impeccably neurotic performance, in Barker's view, one of the best he had got from his actors...

Barker thought deceit legitimate in sexual love and, in the erotic plot, the stealing of the wife its highest moment, for just as he thought desire might undo the bonds of ideology, so in the organised state of the marriage, he saw illicit passion as the stimulus to artistic and tragic invention, in most human beings their imaginative apotheosis... but in *Dead Hands* the tables are cruelly turned, and it is the self-proclaimed urban sophisticate Eff (another of Barker's fortuitous namings...) who comes to grief at the hands of a dead man and his unfathomable mistress... a similar reversal as that which underpins the structure of *He Stumbled* where a physician renowned for his science and sexual mastery falls victim to an erotic plot concocted by two lovers further steeped in eroticism than he is himself... Barker thought Avoth the most skilful of his actors in performing the character of the *batteleur*, the conjuror of the Grand Arcana of the Tarot who, like Barker himself, entertains too many ideas in his head simultaneously and can only sustain his performance by a creative intensity that must eventually – and tragically – exhaust his resources and bring him down... Barker knew and admired a charismatic magician in his locality and had figured him in an early work, as Toplis the mutineer in *Crimes In Hot Countries*... he wrote of him

> *Admire the ageing conjuror*
> *Who has not made the necessary move*
> *From skill to contemplation...*

In Barker's cosmography, the liar/magician, having challenged the authority of the real, has only one destination, and in a profound sense, Death is welcome to him...

Barker had seen Biddy Wells in Colchester's *The Europeans* and saw in her restless energy a natural instinct for his work... like Wicks she had been trained in ballet and had a way with gesture... like her also she could wear clothes and *use* costume to her own advantage... Barker/Kaiser lent her a sexual authority in a range of costumes which emphasised the erotic power of the widow but with a typical inversion he also set against their dark fashion the startling effect of Wells's nakedness, a repeated set-piece which recalls the manner of the string quartet more even than *Wounds To The Face*...

Like nearly all the company's work, *Dead Hands* played an uncomfortable studio at London's Riverside Studios arts complex, a milieu Barker disliked even if its cinema allowed him the luxury of occasionally missing a performance... he routinely watched his own work but suffered the peculiar anxiety associated with it, enjoying it best when there was no audience at all... Riverside was offensive to Barker in the contrary sense to the big civic theatres with their soft furnishings... he no more liked self-consciously artistic milieux than fun palaces... he required theatre to disassociate itself from entertainment, to represent itself spiritually to its public, even perhaps to claim that gravity and ardour which religion once possessed but which the churches in their panic had discarded in favour of the dominant populist ideology of conviviality...

he rarely discovered it and only in places that were not theatres...

31

WHILE *DEAD HANDS* played at Birmingham Rep, Barker asked its artistic director Jonathan Church if he might return to the big stage to mount *The Fence In Its Thousandth Year*, a play with a cast of eight and a chorus of 20 which was to be recruited from amateurs or students in the district... Church was willing to accommodate it for a few days in a slack period... Barker then approached Dee Evans at Colchester to take it there on a similar basis... Barker liked Evans and she had supported him in the past... both directors had accepted The Wrestling School in their theatres in the teeth of the sullen opposition of *the dramaturgy*... a class distinguished by an ethical conformism and a collective appetite for social realism, in effect a police force for the mundane... Barker never wrote for them but he was able on occasion to imitate their game... *The Fence* had a theme which at first sight looked uncommonly *topical* and therefore by the criteria of *the dramaturgy*, hard to dismiss, for topicality was inscribed on the tablets of their faith... mass immigration and the illegal entry of foreigners... the definition and character of 'the nation'... the decay of the frontier... all these subjects were increasingly contentious and Barker had a long-standing fascination with the frontier... with his European, un-English sympathies, he could hardly have felt otherwise, for in Europe the frontier has been the crucifixion of its peoples, a line of sacrifice... but Barker was a dramatist and thought in metaphor... furthermore he was an artist and thought of the image and the stage... whilst Corner was able to exploit the ostensible themes of the work in his applications for funding, Barker's text defied the facile expectations of *the dramaturgy* and the critical class in equal measure...

Wicks played Algeria, the duchess of an unidentified but petty state, wealthy and decadent, a stark contrast to the neighbouring peoples whose appetite for emigration is frustrated by a massive steel fence... thus far the play was redolent of a familiar world, but at once the metaphorical inserted itself... Algeria's private appetites are wholly transgressive and her sex aroused uniquely by transgression... on the one hand she carries on a passionate love affair with a youth assumed to be her nephew, her first secret, on the other she travels routinely to the frontier fence and by night enjoys sex with the foreigner – any one of a competing mass of males – by tossing up her skirts and presenting herself from the rear, a posture both practical and a guarantee of anonymity... the third secret – the real identity of her youthful lover – is revealed early on, when Algeria enters her third marriage and announces to her husband that she reserves her right to continue her liaison with – *her son*... the play's subsequent narrative is entirely concerned with the identity of the father, who it transpires is the blind immigrant who, in an earlier encounter, made Algeria pregnant through the fence... Barker knew well that all barriers are invitations to violation, and his most startling image, the clustering mass of impoverished men fighting for access to the duchess's immaculate body, is typically complex, beautiful and reverberative... in the obscurity, her black costume is suddenly flung up and reveals the dazzling white froth of her petticoats, while the searchlight passes, briefly illuminating the bizarre but passionate act... it is Barker's theatre at its bravest and most compelling... its origins entirely personal to him, for he was transgressive himself... but in its exposition entirely *political*, a classic metaphor in that its meaning extends far beyond its visual content... for the rich exploit the poor both economically and sexually, yet refuse them an identity other than that of the alien... but further, their sexual status depends entirely on *the ban*, which, once removed, concludes the erotic game... when Algeria meets one of her illegal lovers in her own palace, she attempts, and fails, to discover a sexual feeling for him... the fence is all... only the forbidden holds a charge... Barker's exordium for *The Fence* was exemplary in its presentation of all the elements that would later feature significantly in the play... Algeria appears to grieve beside a coffin... the pram which contains her only child is parked adjacently, the nursemaid seated against a wheel, negligently reading while the infant is lifted infinitely slowly out of the pram into the sky on the invisible cable that will later lower it again between Algeria's legs as she gives birth... at the same, scarcely visible velocity the great steel frontier fence descends, against which Algeria will perform her first transgressive act... bowler-hatted court servants pass to and fro to the drones and taps of Jani Cristou interspersed with the wild, abusive shouts that her lovers make on her departure, handkerchief clutched to her mouth... the mist of the frontier clings to the stage... apart from its conspicuous beauty, the exordium to *The Fence* was a shrunken model of the entire work, with its juxtaposition of flesh against wire, class against class, anger, bravery and privilege – for Barker's privileged duchess is a heroine for her pleasures and divinely proud... *The Fence* also contains the scene which for him was the epitome of his dramatic theory as well as his visual and literary style... Algeria, stripped of her authority by a coup and confined to a madhouse, lies on a sordid mattress in a squalid hospital, about to give birth to a child fathered on her by the identical blind foreigner who had fathered her boy lover, Photo, again through a fence, though the fence of the madhouse to which he had traced her... Photo, shocked into infancy by the discovery of his incest (Barker's recollection of Jocasta, and another violated barrier...), sits in a pram with a rattle, with which he sweetly conducts his mother's pain... as Wicks released her deep cries, the rattle twittered and the blind O'Callaghan, louche and infinitely criminal, edged into the room on a stick to luxuriate in his triumphant paternity... but he did not arrive alone... simultaneously and unseen by him, Nigel Hastings's seething but ever-loyal servant Kidney also insinuated himself into the space and, seizing an opportunity, rushed to O'Callaghan and, with the ecstasy of vengeance, proceeded to throttle the old man... but O'Callaghan was unwilling to die... as the men struggled, the baby edged towards its birth, beckoned by its mother's cries... Philip Cumbus, smiling benignly behind dark glasses (for he also is blind...) shook the rattle... Wicks shuddered in her contractions... the men fought a deathly struggle and the baby, a doll and still as a thought, edged into her arms and was comforted into her thighs... all these contrasting actions played out in the jagged soundscape of Ligeti... the child birthed as its father died, and the servant wringing his hands from the strain of strangulation... Scene 15 of *The Fence* is Barker's *Theatre of Catastrophe* encapsulated... its protagonists are both ecstatic and agonised, punished and triumphant at the same time... marginalised survivors, they never yield their passions or ever admit to the collective either their pity or their shame... they are self-invented, self-justified and their entire *raison d'être* is their love, for *The Fence* is nothing if not a love story, and its final image, the duchess undressed by her loyal friend for the eyes of her boy lover – eyes which cannot ever see her beauty – confirmed its origins in its author's passion for his actress as well as his assertion of the incongruity that, according to his metaphysics, defines existence...

32

THE UNCANNY WAS ROUTINE to him and he included it in his thought as an aspect of things, almost a law... he had been with Pointon in the 5th arrondissement on a severe winter's night, and descending steps... he remarked casually that in such heavy snow he almost expected to see wolves return to Paris... as they reached the bottom they passed a statue, of a physician of the 18th century... on its pedestal was the single name *Vulpius*... later, during one of the agonies that punctuated their love affair, Barker walked wildly out of Wicks' house and over fields... as he approached a pair of lonely trees, they wept their leaves, a torrent that had no cause, for it was a still day... he stood under them, hearing the soft rain of their falling, until the branches were entirely bare... he hated cars and walked... the streets held that combination of charm and menace familiar to the *flâneur*... like an animal or bird he felt on guard and this lent him acute powers of observation whilst the lightness of his movements made him sometimes invisible, so people were shocked to discover him... for years he wore steel tips on his heels to announce his presence... he had been born in the city and the city was his milieu... he wrote

> *Leave the city?*
> *But it has my treachery in it*
> *Wild as willowherb on every wall*

The rural idyll had no appeal for him... he thought it subsumed into the heritage racket... his ancestors had been shepherds but he felt only frustration in his attempts to lay a finger on his past...

> *Come to the sickly villages*
> *Where cattle hang from ropes and sheep are propped*
> *To copy grazing...*

He loved relics and remnants even whilst he knew they defied his curiosity, becoming only the substance of new myths, pretexts for annexations...

> *Some bloodless snake lives under the boards*
> *Ancient-eyed*

Infinitely patient

He sheds skins on the parchments

But he also is confined

As all who live off the remnants are

Themselves remnants

In his plays the relic comes to threaten the living with its significance, for it has by virtue of being dead matter a seeming authenticity... it can no longer be corrupted... but it can be appropriated... the head of Bradshaw is used to menace the bankers in *Victory*, and the severed hand of Tovarish acquires a mystical power in *Fair Slaughter*, but it is in *13 Objects* that Barker's emotional relationship with *things* becomes dominant, each object being a focus of painful speculation but also a means of demonstrating the laws of Coercion and Decay that he thought primary... the schoolboy with the ancient camera agonises over what it may have witnessed... the woman with the postcard interrogates it for the precious information it only reluctantly admits... a child's frantic behaviour with its rattle already reveals the instinct to manipulate others... an innocuous spade serves as the focus for a cruel game of life and death... and a coffee-cup becomes the site of desperate nostalgia for an abandoned woman... Barker thought the material detritus of society was imbued with suffering or loss but he shrank from museums unless the museum itself was decayed, subject to the laws it pretended to abolish... and he found rotted museums in obscure places... Slovakia... Poland... Hungary...

33

ARTISTS ARE SOMETIMES REDEEMED by the upheavals of their time... Mayakovsky needed the Bolshevik revolution, even if it led him inexorably to his suicide... he was suffocated by the old regime, even by its *avant-garde*... Barker was oppressed by the cultural dictation of his time but it would not die by violence, if anything he witnessed the intensification of its forms... if he experienced a nausea at social realism very early in his life, the political investment in it ensured it both thrived and was crowned with a legitimacy long after its manifest decay... a grinning corpse propped by the critical regime, it exhaled the moral hypocrisy of an entire era... the realists since Brecht purported to expose the wretchedness of capitalism and thereby to encourage change... Adorno had exposed the lie in this as, unwittingly, Benjamin had, and Benjamin admired Brecht who seemed *active* and therefore charming to intellectuals... Benjamin described the toy donkey in Brecht's study, whose head nodded foolishly and who wore a sign reading 'EVEN I MUST UNDERSTAND...' Barker recoiled from the Brechtian project, with its contempt for its own public, as he recoiled from all simple oppositions on the stage... he knew how deeply implicated all men were in their own oppression... he also sensed the poverty of radical theatre, its preposterous claims to educate and the subsequent grotesque simplifications; he thought the theatre was not *brave* because it feared what might be expressed if the character was truly autonomous; and he watched this moral sclerosis afflict the entire range of its activity... as society became less effectively educated, it invested more and more in educational *initiatives* so that the theatre was drawn deeper into rackets of social amelioration... funding... posts... careers... Barker often spoke of the Soviet system having found its new home here... lying in the public sphere was not confined to politicians... dissent was licensed but only when properly rehearsed... Barker described the moral unanimity as a *treacherous surface* but he could not make headway against it... the dramatist was conventionally thought of as an educator of his public, in Barker's view a pitiful misapprehension of the functioning of art... he had no desire to educate because he thought the stage a sacred place, too complex in its workings for such mundane projects... the ambitions of the English Stage Company and its priggish child, the Joint Stock Theatre group, seemed to him patronising, condescending, patrician in effect... a schoolroom of moralists... his own theatre by contrast disclaimed civility at the outset

> *I bring you an invitation*
>
> *Oh, no, she says, not an invitation*
>
> *Yes*
>
> *We are all so afraid*
>
> *Yes*
>
> *An invitation to hang up the*
>
> *SUFFOCATING OVERCOAT OF COMMUNICATION*
>
> *Hang it up*
>
> *And those with biros write upon your wrist*
>
> *THE PLAY CONTAINS NO INFORMATION*
>
> *Aren't you tired of journalists?*

Oh, aren't you tired of journalists?

No one will hold your hand tonight

Nor oil you with humour

As the swimmer is greased to pass through

Water quicker

No

When the poem became easy it also became poor

When art became mechanised it became an addiction

I lecture!

Oh, I lecture you!

(A terrible storm of laughter.)

Forgive!

Forgive!

(Second Prologue to *The Last Supper*)

Barker knew that the conventions of stage direction, with its emphasis on clarity and communication, qualities seemingly innocuous in themselves, disguised a ruthless political ambition, to force the audience to accept the dictation of the author/director, in other words, to 'get the point...' Barker's practice was the reverse, to create a plethora of possible interpretations and to overwhelm the critical habit... he wanted to abolish the servitude of the audience and lend the public rights of interpretation, an awesome reversal of power relations in an artistic forum where the audience had been trained both to demand and plead for the 'message', as infants cry for the nourishment of milk... Barker knew the audience could only enter the theatre morally clothed – if not suffocated by their ideological garments – but he required them to leave *naked*... this act of *ethical déshabillement* he made the aesthetic of his art of theatre where a new form of tragedy – one which abolished any moral consensus – was the only possible form...

34

ABOVE ALL THINGS Barker wanted to understand the nature of sexual love... its fluctuating dominations and abjections... he sensed in its extreme forms that it both represented and *was* a politics whose arbitrary and irrational impulses menaced the social order... society progressively annexed more and more of the individual, both body and soul... Barker describes the sinister collusions of medicine and politics in his *Death, The One, And The Art Of Theatre*... if man had never owned his own body, which was liable to conscription and punishment at the whim of the state, its parts had never been plundered for collective use... the absolute interchangeability of organs would profoundly alter man's sense of himself in Barker's view, but in the spiritual sphere the rationalists remained frustrated and Barker admired nothing more than the *disastrous liaison*... the conversion of sexual love into pornography might have suited a society that knows the value of commodities as items of control, but Barker sensed that desire was immune to manipulation... in a relatively early work like *Victory* he juxtaposes the quotation of an idealist text by the trembling Scrope with the forced sexual act undergone by his mistress... Barker thought that whereas sex might be shaped by society's fashion editors, psychiatrists and moral engineers, desire would always seep under doors and write itself illicitly… he thought it instinctively *fugitive*… and the irony, that the regimes of liberation detested liberty in the sexual sphere, did not escape him… Robespierre and Lenin believed proletarian virtue extended to the marriage bed, and More's *Utopia* restricted sexuality to the reproductive… if Barker experienced mingled joy and apprehension on the urban street he luxuriated in its erotic exchanges

I saw reflected in five mirrors women
Who jerked their skirts for me
Mauve
Orange
Green
White with a scarlet border
White discoloured by sordidity
And all their knees were bruised:
A bus of tired men stopped
Their lives slopped gallons of monotony
And some were criminal I heard them die
In shot cars shaking their apology
But still I did not raise my eye
From her who drove her fingers deep into her thigh
Forty-seven years her ribs had sailed against
The winter and her breasts were papers pinned
By lawyers to a falling wall
Darling where the church sinks like a slaughtered
Bullock stretch on your heels

I do not ask for cleanliness or that you
Berate your husbands only let me lift you high
In the procession your mouth a red sun
Painted and painted again over the rage cracks

His plays ecstatically affirmed the destructive effects of passion on *values*, the way in which desire eroded responsibility and unpicked *laws*... and if the participants were effectively punished, he saw that as the essence of tragedy... from Katrin and Starhemberg to Algeria and Photo, Barker's texts trace extraordinary devotions whose power is enhanced by their illegality... there is a price to pay and it is solitude, but Barker did not dread it... he was aware he had driven his imagination harder than most men dared... he could not write without hazarding himself, he believed it the duty of the artist to hazard himself and to live with the consequences of painful imaginings...

Knife heart
Have we undone enough now
Unbricked
Unearthed
Unlaced and stretched every part for a sun
To wither?
Knife heart
To find the lakefloor furnished and the
Chambers of the comet hung with wedding
Photographs
Could not shrink your walls tighter
Than they are
We are saddle-hard and angel-proof

Few writers would have driven their imaginations to contemplate such things as the dismemberment of Helen of Troy (*The Bite Of The Night*)... the slaughter of eleven virgins as *an act of love* (*Ursula*)... the sexual extremism of senility and adolescence combined (*The Twelfth Battle Of Isonzo*)... a child killed for *political* reasons (*Let Me...*)... an anatomist driven to dissect himself in public (*He Stumbled*)... even the strange dignity of a torturer (*The Possibilities*)... but meditation on the unforgivable initiated Barker's finest works, and in undressing himself of the comfortable garments of conscience he came to tragedy as few could... for conscience and tragedy are incompatible in the author... it entailed a relentless punishment from the critical police, and he ceased to complain of it because it could only have weakened him

I passed through a door
To where hot lions lay in the sun still as stone
Perhaps stone:
And the eyes of one advised me to adopt their
Lassitude or I would die:
So I watched with them

He could never have discovered the habits of idleness but like any good poet he knew how to watch and to take comfort from watching in itself; something conventional success might have robbed him of because it swallows solitude with its clamour for *presence*... something of Barker's moral independence came from his origins, which he neither vaunted nor apologised for... unlike many of his time, when proletarian credentials were esteemed, he said little about his background unless specifically invited...

he was one of the few writers to have come out of the working class, as he could not have failed to notice at a distinctly middle-class institution like the Royal Court... to have written about it seemed absurd to him, but it lingered in his poetry...

> If some bad angel seized my life from me
> Flying with my heart in his mouth and he
> Parted the fields of brick for my burial place
> I know the hill of aching poverty that he would choose
> The river naked for the estuary
> And legless barbers climbing floors
> Pity their wars and the shorn
> And scented infants of my race

35

THE TENT OF STICKS was held together by goodwill... no one stood to profit by it... the academic critics Rabey, Lamb, Gritzner and others knew they would never be fêted for their insights... it was no different in France... Hirschmuller, Angel-Perez and Kiehl encountered opposition from the usual quarters... Zimmermann and Reitz in Germany... Sakellaridou in Greece... to undertake the defence of Barker was to discover the sort of solitude Barker identified in his plays as the destiny of all who dissented from the moral orthodoxy... but Barker's publishers were men of character and defied the market... Calder was notorious for his independence, his eccentricity, his court appearances... in his list were the greatest names of European literature, some discovered by him, some exposed in English for the first time... the books were hard to find and when you opened them the pages spilled out of the binding... Barker never minded this but he thought the design abysmal, even when his own drawings featured on the covers, but Calder had no visual sense nor the money to employ designers... Barker went to James Hogan, who thought appearance mattered, and got from him beautiful editions... Hogan invested in him from the outset with an immaculate *Ecstatic Bible*, hard-backed in black cloth and with a silk marker, a witty pastiche... such men were rarities and, like Barker, born to opposition...

36

ANIMALS IN PARADISE had gravely hurt the Scandinavian theatres who jointly had commissioned it... two old and once-hostile nations were now joined by a bridge and they thought to use theatre as a trombone to applaud the opening of it... Barker, of neither nation but respected by both, took the commission, which was uncharacteristic... he had not taken a commission since 1981, and that for a community play, anathema to him and explicable only by his passion for a woman who was resident in the distant town... in his violent repudiation of the inhibitions of community theatre he had leapt to the extremes of *Victory*… the woman was the subject of it… the lout Ball describes her…

> *Oh, after I shall write a sonnet, when the fire has gone,*
> *a melancholy piece on how her sad face was like a*
> *pearl, and her hair like silvered weed flowing o'er the*
> *pillow…*

(Victory)

As Barker said, he was made of women…

Who were the Animals, and where was Paradise…? Where they were not self-evident, Barker never explained his titles; they were points of departure, poetic and spontaneous, often invented before the text was written… but if paradise for him was the ecstasy of mutual love, he also knew that men were animals, both beautiful and pitiless… the bridge he was expected to praise as a device of mutuality and civilised exchange becomes a passage of agony in his play, a viaduct of criminality and lost love… Barker thought the performance of it cost him his support in Denmark… he had not liked the production, but it is rare that hostility to *one* production inhibits a career, even when the play has offended national sensibilities… the fact was that *Animals* affirmed – if affirmation was required – Barker's way with both history and morality, and the *dramaturgy* of Malmo recoiled from it no less violently than their London counterparts in the Royal Court and the National Theatre… the artist would not serve the moral enterprise of liberal humanism… he would not affirm the value of progressive ideology… they frowned and were *hurt*…

So in Jean-Michel Déprats's translation the play became *Animaux En Paradis*, and six years later Barker directed it himself... with Wicks, Bertish, O'Callaghan and Moran, who had been the younger son in *Dead Hands*... Barker had proposed a mixed Anglo-French company speaking French, and the young director Guillaume Dujardin, a confirmed *Barkeriste* after directing the French premiere of *Brutopia* in Besançon, had painstakingly set up the exchange... it rehearsed and played in Rouen at Le Théâtre Deux-Rives...

Barker had many assistants but none like Le Brocque, and she was bilingual and a resident of France... she was indispensable, not only in communicating his instructions to the workshop staff but articulating him to the French actors, whose methods were not his own... Jean-Marc Talbot delighted him, saying he saw his function as representing the director on the stage and he did this to his complete satisfaction; he was instinctively an actor of The Wrestling School, Barkerian in mode, vocally versatile, physically brave... others demurred, wanting to *contribute*, a desire Barker greeted with a frown... he spent no time at the table and he asked the actor to realise the role, not to embellish it; he required nothing to be added, whereas the French actors, apart from Talbot, felt the need to *characterise* what was already fully stated on the page... Talbot was triumphant, universally judged to have enhanced his reputation by a superb performance... Barker's dangerous philosopher Machinist was, in Talbot's hands, the epitome of the Barkerian heroic individualist, seductive and provocative, both a doer and a thinker of death... Talbot began by saying he understood nothing of him and later declared the experience had changed his life...

In contradistinction to Jean-Marc Talbot, Christian Pageault could not adapt to Barker's method... for him as for many in the French theatre, text was pretext, and subject to personal taste... opinion... moral attitude... playing another of Barker's dedicated servants, Practice, Pageault wanted to *feel his own* responses to the situations in the scenes and in this sense challenged the authority of the text by choosing to *interpret* it, a presumption difficult to sustain in the author's presence... after discussion with the director he would take refuge in the idea of withdrawing from the rehearsal to *think it over*, in effect an evasion... in his scenes with Wicks he varied his performance nightly, a frustration to her and a symptom of insecurity... he had a strong stage presence, even a magnetism, but Barker wanted it to come out of a commitment to the idea of the scene and not from the persona of the actor... much of the complexity that distinguished the delicate relationship of Wicks' Tenna and Practice was forfeited... her tenderness wasted, the subtle eroticism of her devotion to the body of an old man rendered *bizarre*, and thereby one of Barker's most characteristic passages – the unpredicted and superficially unlikely *liaison* – left unexposed...

Animaux was nevertheless a vindication of Barker's idea of a mixed company and of his direction and design... if there was the conventional suspicion among the French that writers lacked the objectivity to direct their own plays, the production abolished it... the play visited Grenoble, Paris and Le Mans... the company was a happy one... Barker was never a sociable man... society constricted the flow of his thoughts, which under more intimate circumstances flowed in profusion... no one resented the swift departure of the director and his leading actress at the evening's end... to watch his work on stage, to watch his lover perform, was both an ecstasy and an ordeal... they walked for comfort,

His head more blind than wood
In slow seas bumping her shoulder's
Shore...

37

BARKER'S FRIEND the Egyptian poet and film-maker Safaa Fathy wanted to film *He Stumbled...* he himself judged it his best play before *Gertrude – The Cry* and knew it could be told without words – as he wanted all his work filmed – using nothing but natural sound... she wanted to set it in the Mediterranean... he trusted her – she wrote poems to him and had been the first in France to recognise him – but all his landscapes were cold, his imagination thrived in snow and rain and his most loved painters were the Germans of the Renaissance, Dürer, Altdorfer and Baldung-Grien... in Berlin he saw Grien's ink sketch of the execution of Saint Barbara, of 1505... in its swift lines he felt he grasped the whole psychological and ethical spirit of Renaissance humanism, and why it differed so profoundly from the ideological humanitarianism that he found sickly in his own time...

Grien's drawing reverses the order of prominence in conventional images of Christian martyrdom... the focus has been shifted from the saint to the executioner, an old man without malice who gently turns the saint's shoulder in order that he might deliver an accurate blow... the effect is to eliminate all trace of that moral attitude common to most descriptions of martyrdom, visual or literary... even Dürer's rendering of the same subject shows the executioner as a posturing lout... Barker knew that the same scene described in his own time would shriek with moral outrage, whereas Grien's humanism stressed the human being in the professional killer and showed him as an inhabitant of a world which for all its cruelties still allowed for sympathy, even at the point of death... when he came to paint the subject himself, Barker shifted the terms of the composition yet further, as he had violently reordered the Judith narrative in *Judith*... in his version the executioner is an apprentice and a woman herself, anxious but determined... she is watched by an ageing professional, willing her to succeed... the tension of Barker's version contrasts with the placidity of Grien's, but both artists share a common refusal to impose an interpretation on the events described... they deny their public the facile pleasures of associating itself with the received wisdom of the culture...

38

DISCARDING HOPE from his ethical system enabled Barker to discover tragedy... he became *hope-less*... but this was not synonymous with pessimism, a critical notion he thought valueless like its opposite... to be *hope-less* enabled him to excavate where others might have hung back, unwilling to expose a cherished house of attitudes to the risk of disintegration... Barker did not understand compatibility in the dramatic or the moral world... things collided... collision was the essence of human experience... he had faith in himself as an artist but as nothing else... never as a teacher... never as *exemplary*...

I am not better than the tall police
Who locked sad secrets in their rooms
But clad their heels in iron and stood
In slanting rain their capes shining
Like knives

Even the most passionate sexual encounters were threatened by the inexorable facts of coercion and decay... in his private existence and in his texts he nevertheless affirmed ecstasy as the only riposte to life's laws, but ecstasy with another, a defiant *duality*... a perfection of the 'we' outside the hounding conformity of the collective... sometimes there was defeat...

The clay in you
The shoulders and the womb clayful
An excellent weight
And in the words this same sodden aggregate

Of time's unfaltering anger
I could hear the ploughing and the dying
In them

But also triumph…

Let my hand down
I have the dimensions of your belly
Thumb-to-fingertip one woman width
Your sharpened hips might be the tools of
An antiquity:
Let my hand down
The proudest digit of my four will trace
Your hair swirl to its cleft
And at that gate wait for words
To take their precedence:
I am educated in this nothingness
And teach nothingness:
That is the verdict of your going eyes
As the floors of you rise

Only a tragic sensibility could discover in loss and in the thwarting of dreams a melancholy beauty that kept Barker from despair and at the same time enabled him to claim for the most terrible of his tragedies that they were spiritually *necessary* – his whole justification for his theatre… for him theatre could never be ambitious enough in the complexity of its themes, its excesses never too great to satisfy the human longing for some sign that pain was not disorder but *necessity*…

Dead trucks climb
I like their whispering with the bloodless
Their tyres black as lipstick:
A horse urged our gaolbreak with white eyes
But I failed him
Leaving him to gallop his whole life between
White ribbons

The ever-running racehorse, destined to die of exhaustion from his pursuit, was a Barkerian metaphor comparable to the illogical but defiant gesture of the conjuror – neither is instructed by his experience and both exhibit a supremely wilful manner with reality – neither can or will reach an accommodation with the *facts*... Wittgenstein's bleak assessment that 'the world is all that is the case' might be an admonition to the metaphysicians neither to struggle nor to dream, but for the Barkerian heroine, pride alone makes accommodation with such banality impossible... perhaps the world is simply not sufficient for the searching women of Barker's oeuvre, just as the male protagonists like Dancer of *Hated Nightfall* elect always to 'kick to the finish' rather than submit to some final placidity at the door of death, or like Claudius in *Gertrude – The Cry* who requires to be put to death by the woman who obsesses him as soon as he recognises this to have been the secret of their passion, and so declines a life of tranquillity and reflection...

39

BARKER'S *DEATH, THE ONE AND THE ART OF THEATRE*, for all its metaphysical speculation, was a statement of the fact, first articulated in a Paris interview, that he did not know the theatre and the theatre did not know him... a subtle re-situating of himself in the world which concluded his relation with the existing dispensation but, far from marking his departure, proceeded to distinguish what he now identified as *the theatre* – a form of entertainment decadent even where it claimed to be most radical – from his own *art of theatre*, an entirely different practice of a spiritual kind, unethical but tragic and distinguished by a supreme *unknowingness* – a passionate rejection of the enlightenment practice of all English theatre, with its political triteness and conventional outrages... Barker did not write comedy but he had a profoundly comic sense as all tragedians do... he was mischievous with his enemies whilst simultaneously taking pains to identify the profound schisms that lay inside theatre's complacent tolerances... Barker was himself not tolerated and he needed to know why, if only to spare himself the destructive bitterness that might have spoiled his art... he understood that to live without enemies was impossible, that even the hermit offends... he had written a poem, *Refuse To Dance*, early in his career, and it identified that resistance which was needful to anyone who declined to be manipulated by populist culture, a resistance which would inevitably be deemed churlish just as an individual who declines to dance is regarded with contempt by those who, for the sake of that collective coercion dignified by the name of *solidarity*, are prepared to *dance badly*...

40

BARKER LIVED IN ONE HOUSE for 30 years and it contained relics both of his own life and the lives of others... the correspondence of a prisoner in Siberia... pairs of his lover's high-heeled shoes... dead men's clothing... toys and photographs, always photographs of places he could never identify, picked up on stalls in Vienna or Ljubljana and a source of pain to him, for the photograph hurts with its pitiful relationship with decay, its perpetual singing of loss... and he had a dolls' house where decay was, if not stopped, made metaphor, furnished with figures and furniture made by him and each room telling a fragment of a life... profligacy... marriage... solitude... he had known all three, and some brief, transient relationships continued to fill him with amazement long after... sometimes when the woman was dead...

I recollect a woman who placed a sheet
On you when you had satisfied her
And calling friends said tiptoe near
This is my brief boy...

The lightest room was filled with paintings... it was hard to move for them, they slumped against walls like hospital patients, narrowing the space left for the easel and the paints... he had sold many, to national collections and to individuals, but he painted more than he sold and they encroached... among them the massive triptych *IRA Bits*, a crushing rebuke to political terrorism, with its dismembered trunks, standing or lying in groups... and always the female form, most often Wicks, whose hips and limbs he could reproduce swiftly with brush or ink...

He might have lived anywhere, for it is the writer's privilege to choose his place, and Barker was anyway in exile in his own country, effectively... he was intimate with Vienna, Paris and Copenhagen, all cities loved by him and each with its favoured café; above all he loved the Hawelka and entered it with the gratitude a son might feel entering his father's room, with its worn and loved furniture... but he kept to one place whose character was at odds with his own and deliberately, for what offended him stimulated him and Brighton was simultaneously chic and sordid, idle, criminal and insincere... always he walked it, and he had been a student there, married there and brought up children... it remained incorrigibly false, a city of façades which not even the heaving winter sea could dignify... and he had a foreboding that its ostentatious poverty (never a contradiction in this city, and a sign of its *modernity*) would one day engulf him...

This river of unhealing
I have walked here too often and with unfree eyes
Paying tax to the blasphemers:
I stand inside my ribs and from my femur
Hangs my murderer and from my wrist
A too-bright flower:
Listen it is unwise to dance at me

Doing the killing motion on the kerb
I turned away a wife and night breeds
Storms in me of ice and sharktooth

Criminality held no fascination for him and Brighton is a place of criminals, but he liked the tradesmen whose tenacity impressed him, especially the ironmongers... his father had worked with tools and Barker admired his way of handling them... the effect of their working on the skin... he remarked on the beauty of his father's hands and how work if anything enhanced it... he was familiar with these knife-sharpeners and took their names for characters... what *he* did remained a mystery to them... Barker was in every way a European and knew its cities, its palaces and its cemeteries, its cathedrals and its battlefields, but he chose obscure routes... few things afforded him more pleasure than to arrive in an obscure port aboard a ferryboat whose unprofitable and infrequent service had somehow been overlooked... his great overcoat smothering his lover as they watched the lorries and their trailers explode onto the quay...

Dujardin identified Barker's theatre as a traumatic break with liberal humanism in the cultural world, a rupture with a calcified but self-perpetuating system which justified itself by its posture of critique but was in effect a redundant, decayed aesthetic... Barker himself thought such a theatre was sustained only by a Soviet-style bureaucracy and an ingrained anti-intellectualism which he had always taken as characteristic of the English but was no longer confined to them... the moral unanimity of the European intelligentsia was a deafening drumbeat and the further Barker invested in the tragic form, the greater the price he paid in isolation... this was no less than he expected for tragedy cannot pay dues to ideology, its nature repudiates it... but what multiplied Barker's offence and enhanced his contradiction to the rule was his development of a performance style which contrasted starkly with governing conventions... a style which furthermore obliterated the suffocating domesticity of social realism and was integrated in every department of its practice... in this he was supported by a dedicated core of actors who shared his sense they were reclaiming theatre for a different and darker purpose... together they bypassed realism with apparently effortless ease, the consequence of a profound discipline and – on Barker's part – an aesthetic programme he had arrived at by a rigorous contemplation of theatre and the moral/political world which licensed it...

Success in its familiar form could only have damaged Barker, for it comes roped to celebrity, which he thought a crippling deformation of good repute... his imagination was in any case too vigorous to be snared in the reproductive process of success with its sordid metabolisms... he did not want to see his work played and replayed in circumstances which could only diminish it, even if he knew no work of art could ever be 'possessed' by its creator... he had seen many versions of his texts, sometimes savagely manipulated, even in one instance by a theatre company in Brussels whose very title could only have alerted his most profound suspicions... The 'Theatre of Utopia' proceeded to behave in a predictably Utopian manner – by annexing, distorting and simplifying Barker's deeply-layered *The Europeans* in order to wring a 'progressive' political message from its simmering contradictions... to those of us who witnessed it, there could have been no starker revelation of the sickly practices of a 'directors' theatre' which blindly obliterated texts for political and moral ends of the most banal kind, a manifestation of a systematised morality which dreads to be opposed...

One damp afternoon in London a conference took place around Barker's work and it included a showing of his short play *Pity In History*, which had, unusually, been televised... the part of a mortally injured cook, ranting in his dread of death, was played by Ian McDiarmid with characteristic energy... unnoticed, a vagrant ex-soldier had come in off the street and began vociferously complaining at the play's failure to respect the cardinal rule of social realism, namely that things must be shown 'as they are...' This aged veteran, his chest dazzling with campaign medals, discovered Barker and harangued him with the fact that 'men don't die like that...' Barker was rarely embarrassed by such accidents, road-smashes of the fictional world, but he felt acutely the resentment of the old man, who had seen at first hand what Barker only dared to imagine... at the same time he sensed the multiplicity of intentions played out in their confrontation, for he himself would yield nothing to experience, whereas the old soldier wielded his still-smarting memories as a weapon by means of which he could exert authority... as Barker revealed in every work he wrote, pity and pain are nothing if not infinitely *exploitable*... the argument was incapable of resolution since Barker never claimed to be a realist and knew perfectly well that men on the rim of death rarely deliver diatribes even if he thought it *not impossible*... all the same it was a vivid demonstration of how profoundly Barker violated public tolerance in his pursuit of a theatrical form, for what he required of his audience was the *sacrifice* of those gratifications associated with the social-realist theatre, including, as in this instance, the *right* to be recognisable, in order that the *instincts* of theatre, with its artistic as opposed to political truths, might be admitted to prominence, with all the exhilarations and dismay that this involves...

41

BARKER HAD DRAMATISED the decay of political orthodoxies, as well as the decay of the individuals associated with them, in plays as varied as *Victory*, *The Power Of The Dog* and *The Bite Of The Night*, and he had described the systematisation of liberal humanism and its hardening into a *regime*... the authoritarians who masquerade behind their virtues in *Gertrude – The Cry* and *The Fence In Its Thousandth Year* are the enemies of love no matter how they advertise their attachment to sex, now a commodity of gratification and potentially an instrument of social control... if Marx had characterised religion as an opiate of populations, the same judgement could be applied to pornography and its icons in the entertainment industry... the stripped body is a *lingua franca* of a spiritually barren and desensitised society, but in Barker's theatre it acquired an emblematic status beyond the erotic... in theatre the living body has a hazardous potential unavailable to the makers of film, and nakedness is its crisis point...

Barker-as-Kaiser was careful to dress his women with an elegance that bore high status... he had read of the Spanish court of the 17th century and wanted to imitate its disciplines on the stage, so that stillness carried authority and, as a consequence, all movement was revelation, of irritation, dread or partiality... Barker frequently instructed an actor to work a certain gesture into a moment, even the removing of a glove, or the folding of an umbrella... his fastidious clothing of the body, above all the female body, implied, invited, even demanded, the revelation of the nakedness that lay beneath it... it was embedded in the spectacle, a calculation that was inevitably an impatience... in his play for marionettes *The Swing At Night* Barker took this anticipation further, as he could do only with string puppets, making the female protagonist, a murderer of men, transparent, a model of Perspex, so that revelation was simultaneously absence... Wicks provided the voice of Klatura; McDiarmid spoke for Otto, her complicit child... Barker saw nakedness both as pity and power... whereas the stripped body of the precocious Gay in *The Bite Of The Night* oscillates with authority and its abolition...

If I am naked and you are not, what then?
One of us has the advantage, but who...?

in *Animaux En Paradis* the ancient servant undresses under the gaze of his young mistress and stands among his fallen clothes dignified by her desire but also a spectacle of the decline of the human body... this was the moment of anxiety Barker so cherished in his writing and staging... Wicks lay on the floor like a child, head in hands, curious, aroused, adoring... the audience experienced the frisson of horror caused by the juxtaposition of age and beauty, power and submission, and suffered the tension of not knowing where they might be taken next, for Barker had a reputation for dangerous liaisons even if he was scrupulous never to swamp his stage with the bathos of a 'realistic' sexual act... the moment of lingering wonder, a perfect stillness but for Wicks' slowly moving leg, endured until Laurent Savalle, playing the husband of Wicks, entered the room, a third party to this pitiful incongruity, and without anger gazed on their mutual gaze... nakedness is the great secret of the stage, and the stage an art of secrecy according to Barker, transmitting its meanings by routes so indirect he could scarcely bear to examine them for dread of making laws out of their exquisite evasions... in the deafening racket of an industrialised culture, he thought tragedy operated beneath the norms of communication...

> *In the rush of songs how can it be said*
> *THIS fell into my ear this perfect call?*
> *We do not heed the announcers their speech*
> *Is a traffic but to hear the unloud?*
> *We do not kneel now or know how to kneel*

In the complex relations of stage and audience, he knew the public had to renounce in order to acquire... to give up in order to find...

42

These last opinions:

Winged toys falling among trees:

And the rooms emptied of rage fill instead

With faith or liquor

IN HIS POETRY Barker studied loss but his stage was a place of stress and collision, a site of passionate living even where the characters – by strictly realistic standards – are beyond the age of activity... Isonzo is 100 years old but his crippled body is a cage in which his spirit paces like a tiger... if he can no longer engender love, he will caper in its ruins... Mrs Gollancz and The Priest in *The Ecstatic Bible* outlive the centuries in their undesired immortality but yield nothing to wisdom, and Pope Pius in *Rome* will never succumb to death so long as he can glimpse the arse of his mistress, albeit his heart has long ago stopped beating... all these characters, pairs of lovers or solitary *déracinés*, robbed by political powers and condemned to wander a spoiled landscape until they die, invest in their emotions and their instincts in a manner which can only be compared to *prayer*, which, uttered against a wall, comes back as echo yet sustains...

Barker had never even in his most political phase believed in *the correct course,* and his first major work *Claw* saw its hero drowned without conceding to a political education... error fascinated Barker, self-evident truths bored him...

I will not cease to love the wrongthinkers

Or linger on bare stairs to hear

The cries of the clinging:

I said no to her I swung this no of iron

Against her brow

Now the police pass with their urgent music

A million clouds have marched over my room

Yet the mirrors are not mutinous

They do not clamour for improved reflections yet

Acts of uneducated faith he found beautiful, the more so if they were stubbornly adhered to, and there is a greater affection for The Old Woman's misapprehensions in *A Medal* (*13 Objects*) than for The Soldier's bitter analysis of his own bravery, a short scene that reveals the deep stresses that groan like steel cables beneath his work, binding the incongruities together…

There was a barracks in the snow

Where soldiers dreamed of blood and mothers

I went with a little flag to show

My loyalty so when they died they'd know

A child had blessed their cause

Barker could never reduce his theatre to exercises in what is patronisingly termed 'consciousness-raising', a dubious exercise in his opinion, even in revolutionary contexts, and fatuous in media-fixed democracies… he was nauseated by the theatre of demonstration, where self-appointed teachers disseminate their superior wisdom to a public they deem too susceptible to lying… he wanted to deepen the anxiety of his public, not to relieve it by substituting one parcel of sentimental fallacies for another... the theatre of journalists was forever *announcing* and the social realists *told* only in order to *affect*... in tragedy and through his own way with it Barker divested himself of every moral discipline except that attaching to the production itself... he lent complexity to his public not as a gesture of solidarity to increase their resistance to the organisation of opinion, but because he could write in no other way...

43

BARKER'S ARTISTIC PERSONALITY was one of extremes... he could write simply

In the absence of rewards
To lift the same pots and wash them
To hang them and hear them moan on nails

Or describing the departure of soldiers

Mothers combed their hair
Crying oh let me
And some had brushed the loosed hair
Of the mothers
In dim kitchens
Saying my dear one

But also in cascades of imagery half-surreal

I shone a copper tray
The sun beat it with his fist
I shone it to transport one glass
Sycophantically
The whole length of a path
Black with the ash of ships
A funeral path
My costume itched
I rolled on bad eyes
Llamas stared from the ribs
Of cattle wet with sudden mist
It was wholly necessary
THERE you shouted with a damaged
Mouth
THERE
I did not slip in the black fluids
A dog ran near so hot with memory
I smelled his fur

At the heart of his creative nature was an inextinguishable *disobedience* which, if it rendered him uncomfortable to institutions and made institutions intolerable to him, also drove his imagination, preserving it from stagnation on the one hand and *service* on the other… never a mere mutineer, Barker sensed decay in forms and narratives and in his recoil from them found himself in new places – new places sometimes very old – as once he had fled for his life down sordid city streets in dead of night and, shaking off his pursuer at last, discovered himself in an oasis of lush vegetation, incongruous and placid, and fell asleep there…

he was of his time but also distinctly alien to it… of his country but always foreign to it… so English in appearance he nearly parodied it with his high forehead and narrow jaw, but never sharing its culture… he had English manners when he *wanted* them – itself surely a contradiction and an aspect of his disguise – so that strangers could not associate the man with what he wrote… manners and clothes were elements of a deceit which he both enjoyed and yet was necessary to him…

44

BARKER NEEDED THE SECRET, both in his life and in his art. Any revolution, with its clamour for revelation, disclosure and the breaking of the boundary, could only have identified him as an enemy, just as the populist democracy under which he lived also recognised his dissent and exiled him, for its system was a masquerade of revolutionary regimes and faked their rhetoric, with its trombone of 'equality' and 'the people' its bass drum… it also boomed its passion for 'transparency', and its media, effectively the people's police, purported to be critical but was symbiotic in effect… heir of Marat and Robespierre, it was bent on the elimination of the private sphere, and, in classic revolutionary mode, found scientists and artists queuing to legitimise its ostensibly democratic but conformist ideology…

Barker knew the history of Europe and knowing it felt justified in inventing it, for the system invented and reinvented it itself under his eyes... his histories were excavations of the buried or concealed but never written for enlightenment... the fate of the Romanoffs in *Hated Nightfall*... the undocumented life of a republican widow in *Victory*... the identity of the Unknown Soldier in *The Love Of A Good Man*... and the alternative account of Marie Antoinette in *The Gaoler's Ache For The Nearly Dead*... all for Barker ecstasies of historical untruth whose own truths made *truth* humble in the presence of emotion, as the party policeman Denadir finds in *Hated Nightfall* and consequently is killed because he himself can kill no longer... and in his interrogation of the classics it is always the secret which attracts Barker to the play, if only to deepen its mysteries... the inexplicable absence of Lear's queen gives rise to *Seven Lears*, and it is the great secret of *Hamlet* – the passion of Gertrude for Claudius – that enabled Barker to write his greatest work on love... Barker's philosophical master was Adorno, a Marxist and materialist until he came to speak of art... and his theologian was Meister Eckhart, who knew God was not there and made faith from His absence... Barker learned from them to speak of the unspeakable and to look where nothing seemed to be...

Have you an eye for the cracks?
Some have
Some hear the birds fall and mark how
Every wall is thinner following the storm

45

I WATCHED BARKER REHEARSE IN PIMLICO... he would rehearse only in this building, which had not been painted nor repaired for 50 years... when it rained they put out buckets and rehearsed around the buckets... in summer, Avoth killed the wasps with his fists... Barker walked here from the great station, stopping on the way for a coffee and one of his beloved *Gitanes*... the café was on a square, and buses left all the time for Cracow, Zagreb, Ossiek... the waiters were Portuguese, the queues were Poles or Serbs... he loved the Poles, for their politeness and their passions... the Serbs for their history... the Polish director Jerzy Klesyk had shown *The Possibilities* and *Judith* to the Parisians... Barker and Wicks were invited to Paris for a conference on Barker, and Wicks in a close-fitting suit of grey leather read the 'grey' speech from *Gertrude – The Cry*, the first time it had been heard in public... the audience were transfixed by her... in the following debate Klesyk said, before 300 people, that Barker's work kept him from suicide... such compliments a writer never forgets... yet he wrote to 'help' nobody but himself... he thought such effects incidental even if tragedy saved by telling the worst... no one, man or woman, could love another in his opinion, if they did not first love themselves, it was the pre-condition of giving, and he applied this to art which had first to serve its maker before it could acquire the power to serve others... a law he applied to his *mise-en-scène*, where things frequently occurred which were *comprehensible* only to him but which contributed to the profound beauty of the whole...

meaning had to be made from what emerged... for Barker it was the deepest power of theatre that it resisted coercion... that what the public takes from great plays is rarely what the maker of the play intends... like him it was fundamentally disobedient and, however plastic, overflowed the *mould*...

In the rehearsal room were faded photographs of dead boy scouts smiling for the camera... the cupboards spilled remnants of old Bibles and score-cards of darts teams long-dispersed... sometimes the police crouched in the window to observe the movements of the criminals, but silently in order not to disturb the actors who also spoke strange languages... sometimes Barker left to go upstairs where other actors tried out costumes... an ancient and untuned piano acted as a rack for his black wools and dazzling taffetas... felt hats... the swirls of boned corsets... dark coats sweeping the floor... and from the window he saw the pitiful yet perfect garden made by the melancholy caretaker... etiolated plants in a bizarre assortment of cut-down plastic containers, as if a choir of sickly children whimpered in a wasteland of silenced industry... from this chaotic and incongruous building, old and choked with its own detritus, came Barker's hard and exquisite productions, dark and light as steel blades in night-time... he required the past and its remnants nearly as addiction, but drew out of it an absolute modernity which in a faithless age had faith's exhilarations and its agonies...

STARHEMBERG: *Nothing I say will be true...*
everything I say I will later retract... the apparent
logic of my position is only the dressing of flagrant
incompatibilities...

EMPRESS: *Obviously... and that is why we trust you,*
Starhemberg...

(*The Europeans*)